Giants of the Keyboard

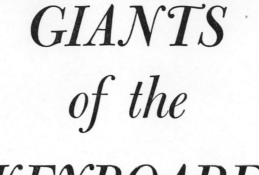

GIANTS
of the
KEYBOARD

Victor Chapin

J. B. Lippincott Company

PHILADELPHIA   NEW YORK

TO ANNE HULL

Contents

Giants of the Keyboard

Prélude

THE pianoforte, which actually was invented in 1711, was regarded in the ensuing six decades as more of a curiosity than anything else. Like so many other important innovations, it was not really used until it was definitely needed. So long as musicians performed only in small ballrooms or salons, the existing keyboard instruments sufficed. But as soon as public concerts came into existence and musicians found themselves performing in larger rooms, the need for a louder, stronger, and more subtle keyboard instrument became evident. Fortunately, the pianoforte was there, waiting in the wings, so to speak. When it finally was presented to the general public, in the year 1769, it was not an instrument that bore much resemblance to the one we know today as the grand piano. Though the basic principle by which it operated was the same as it is today, it did not look the same, sound the same, or have the same extended range.

Nobody had looked upon the keyboard instruments as suitable for solo performances before the end of the seventeenth century, except in England, where composers of the Tudor and Stuart periods found delight in creating pieces for accomplished ladies and gentlemen to perform upon the virginals or clavichord. However, it can be said that in general the need for the pianoforte was created by a new public outside the aristocracy that began to listen to music in public places and by the promotion of the keyboard instruments from the status of accompanist to that of soloist. Even so, the solo recital, at which one musician plays one instrument during an entire concert, was unknown until the early nineteenth century and unestablished until well into that century.

We know that music has always existed and that it achieved complexity and sophistication in the civilizations of the Greeks, the Hebrews, the Chinese, the Hindus, and the Arabs. And yet, our ancestors tended to believe that music was an exclusive product of our civilization. Many of them, through no fault of their own, even believed that no music of importance was created before 1685, the year in which three of our first great composers were born. Though Johann Sebastian Bach, George Frederick Handel, and Domenico Scarlatti were, no doubt, the first real giants of music, they were not the creators of styles and traditions but the men who, through their genius, brought the style and tradition of baroque music to their culmination.

Music in the Western world was for many centuries largely vocal and mainly liturgical. However, folk songs and simple pieces for the lute, recorder, viols, or dulcimer have been discovered from early medieval times. The composers of the Renaissance brought polyphonic vocal music to a high degree of complexity and beauty. Opera, an Italian creation, began in the late sixteenth century as a kind of musical-dramatic recitation and achieved entity of form and content in the mid-seventeenth century in the works of Claudio Monteverdi, the first great operatic composer.

Historians, sociologists, and psychologists have often commented upon and attempted to explain the fact that music was the last of the arts to develop and mature. When Bach, Handel, and Scarlatti were born, Dante had been dead for 364 years, Shakespeare for 69 years, and Michelangelo for 121 years. All the great cathedrals of Europe already had been built. Perhaps it was natural, or at least inevitable, that the art and science of sound should be the last of man's chief concerns. Music, after all, is an abstraction, and abstractions are luxuries. No wonder then that music began with the human voice and for many years could not be enjoyed for itself but had to be connected with some familiar mythological, historical, or religious meaning.

In the seventeenth century, as in preceding and subsequent centuries, musicians were dependent on patronage. They were at the mercy of princes, either of the court or of the church. The best (or sometimes merely the cleverest) of them secured official appointments as directors of music for a king or a prince, a cardinal or a bishop. Every church and court of any importance in Europe had its official musicians. The *maestro di capella* to a prince or a cardinal was an important and usually fortunate personage, though more often than not he was considered little better than a servant. The circumstances in which even the most successful musician lived were perilous. He was totally subservient to his patrons, subject to their whims and fashions, involved in intense rivalries, and expected to provide new and interesting music whenever it was demanded. In those days, the people who listened to music, in church or at court, were in the habit of hearing only new works and were apt to be annoyed if presented with music they had heard before.

The human voice was the great instrument of the seventeenth century, as it was to be for most of the eighteenth. Public taste, which was that of the ruling aristocracy, was for opera and, because these people had to go to church, for vocal music of a religious nature. Though the operas familiar to us today, with one or two exceptions, were all composed no earlier than the end of the eighteenth century, when Gluck and Mozart brought about a revolution in opera by making it truly theatrical, the rage for opera (or, at least, for singing) began in the seventeenth century. Instrumental music played a poor second to opera until the middle of the eighteenth century. Instruments were considered important only as accompaniments to the human voice. There had been times and places in which instrumental music had enjoyed some popularity before the time of Bach, Handel, and Scarlatti, particularly in England, where the Fitzwilliam Virginal Book was collected in 1625. Henry Purcell of England, François Couperin of France, Arcangelo Corelli of Rome, and Antonio Vivaldi of Venice were the first great instrumental composers. They were all active during the late seventeenth century.

It was during this same period, which just preceded the age of Bach, Handel, and Scarlatti, that the stringed instruments reached their ultimate development. The great instrument makers of Cremona, particularly the three members of the Stradivari family, the four Guarnieris, and the four Amatis, as well as the earlier Gasparo da Salò of Brescia, perfected the construction of violins, violas, and cellos. It is the instruments of these masters, all made between 1550 and 1743, that are desired by string players today. Nobody since has succeeded in making instruments of comparable quality.

The piano, on the other hand, is a modern instrument that developed slowly over a period of two and a half centuries. It had predecessors, of course. In fact, there is evidence that the Greeks possessed some sort of keyboard instrument, for a clay figurine of the second century A.D. that was found at Corinth depicts an instrument with nineteen discernible keys. This became known as the *hydralus,* or Greek organ. In Christian history, the use of the organ can be traced to the fifth or possibly the fourth century A.D., and so it can be projected that our modern organ had its origins in the Greek *hydralus,* which, in turn, may have derived from some similar instrument of an older civilization. We know from a Norman sculptured relief of the tenth or eleventh century that a kind of hand organ, predecessor of the hurdy-gurdy, was in existence then. At the same time, another instrument, the monochord, used mostly for acoustical experiments, had gained currency. This instrument, which was called the Pythagoras because it probably was handed down from the

Greeks, consisted of a single string stretched over a resonance box. The player controlled pitch with a movable
bridge that was pressed by hand. It was through the use of
this monochord that Guido d'Arezzo and other musical sci-
entists of the early middle ages were able to determine pitch
relations and begin their experiments with musical notation
in an effort to preserve the plain chant of the Church. In the
eleventh century, more complex monochords with two or
more strings were developed.

The monochord appears to have been the direct ancestor
of the clavichord. A carved figure of the early fifteenth century in the church of St. Mary's of Shrewsbury in England
represents a man playing a small, box-like stringed instrument that has a keyboard with seven or eight keys. A manuscript discovered in Weimar, Germany has a pen and ink
miniature of an instrument called the clavichordum, which
has eight long and sixteen short keys with twelve strings in
evidence. Unfortunately, these two visual documents do not
show us how the actions of these instruments worked,
whether by quills, thongs, tangents, or something else. Another manuscript found at Ghent in Belgium illustrated a
recognizable clavichord of the early fifteenth century.

The harpsichord developed from a medieval stringed instrument that existed in several variations and is referred to
in the writings of Boccaccio as the cembalo and in those of
Chaucer as the sautrie. The clavichord being a simpler instrument than the harpsichord, it probably evolved into its
final form at an earlier date.We know that the chromatic keyboard, which had eight keys to the octave and was made to
conform to the scale developed by Guido d'Arezzo, was in use
during the fifteenth century. The harpsichord developed
from the psaltery, which was the English name given to the
instrument that existed in both dulcimer and zither form.
Since the oldest harpsichord in existence (the Roman clavicembalo by Geronimo of Bologna in the Victoria and Albert
Museum in London) dates only from 1521 and the oldest
clavichord (the Manicordo of Eleanora di Montalvo at Flor-

ence) from 1659, we do not know exactly how the two instruments evolved. There are records indicating that the
thong-type action of the harpsichord was in use in the fifteenth century. The word spinet, which was applied to earlier forms of the harpsichord, may have derived from the
Italian *spina* (thong) or from the name of Giovanni Spinetti,
a Venetian instrument maker of the late fifteenth century.
During the sixteenth century, several types of spinetta were
developed, all of them portable and of limited range. The
first spinet with legs was built in the seventeenth century.
The instrument that we recognize as the harpsichord, with
an upper piano keyboard and a lower forte keyboard, was
invented about 1640 by Jan Couchet, a member of a family
of instrument makers, the Ruckers of Antwerp, who had
previously developed several versions of the double keyboard
and introduced the use of stops. In the eighteenth century, it
was the harpsichords made by the Rucker family that were
in the greatest demand. At the same time, the instrument
was developed further by English builders such as Jacob
Kirchaman and Burckhard Shudi (both Germans originally), who added the use of pedals. It was an Englishman,
Roger Plenius, who invented the harp effect, produced by
muting the string vibration with a small piece of leather,
that gave the harpsichord its eventual name. Plenius also
has some claim to being the one who first built a pianoforte
in England.

The harpsichord, which used to be known more generally
as the cembalo (from *gravicembalo* or *clavicembalo*) is
more accurately described as a keyboard psaltery, rather
than a keyboard harp, as its name implies. The instruments
known as the virginals are smaller harpsichords that operate
with the same mechanism. The shape of the harpsichord—
wing shaped—served as the model for the eventual grand
piano. In larger harpsichords, there were from two to four
strings (wire or gut) that were sounded by the action of upright jacks standing between the strings. Each of these jacks
was equipped with a quill or leather thong that plucked the

strings and with a soft damper to check their vibration. Pressing a key raised the corresponding jack and twanged the strings.

In some instruments, both leather thongs and quills were used on the jacks to give variety to the tone, and eventually separate keyboards were installed for the jacks with quills and those with thongs (piano and forte keyboards). Stop levers to change the tension of the strings and so change the tone were features of some larger harpsichords. The range of the harpsichord differed with the size of the instrument, but it usually was of from four to six octaves.

During the sixteenth century, the harpsichord became an important instrument of the orchestra, and it was the harpsichordist (then known as cembalist) who acted as conductor, though in those times the art of the conductor was restricted to giving cues and supplying the necessary harmonic underpinnings to the work being played. The cembalist was expected to fill in the appropriate harmonies from the figured bass (*basso continuo*) that was all the composer indicated in his score.

The clavichord, or keyboard polychord, was essentially a portable instrument, rectangular in shape, that was set upon a table. Its shape later became the model for the square piano. The earliest clavichords had a range of two and a half octaves but by 1700 went to four or five. The strings were extended behind the keyboard and parallel to it, over a sounding board. The action consisted of a brass tangent behind each key. When a key was struck, the upright tangent was forced against a string, sounding a vibration that could be controlled and given vibrato by a rocking motion of the finger on the key. When the tangent hit the string, the pitch was determined by its location on the string. A damper limited the vibrations of the string so that the wrong overtones would not be sounded. The damper strips automatically killed the note sounded as soon as the key was released.

The harpsichord had a stronger and richer but more metallic sound, while the clavichord was capable of greater subtlety and gradation of tone and so of more expressiveness, which is why Bach came to prefer it as a solo instrument. However, the harpsichord remained the instrument of the orchestra until that time when the pianoforte took its place, which was not long before composers began to fill in the harmonies in their orchestrations and so dispensed with the need for a keyboard instrument in the orchestra, except for special effects.

Musicians had longed for a stronger and at the same time more subtle instrument for years before the pianoforte was invented. Several unsuccessful attempts were made to combine the clavichord and the harpsichord into one instrument before Bartolommeo Cristofori developed his pianoforte action which, though it was of revolutionary importance, did not achieve any real acceptance for fifty years or more.

Cristofori, an instrument maker in the employ of the Medici princes of Florence, began experimenting with new keyboard actions about 1702 and finally perfected his invention in 1711. The Cristofori action introduced the principle of striking the strings with a hammer instead of plucking them with a thong, quill, or tangent.

For many years, there was confusion about who actually invented the pianoforte. However, Cristofori's claim is now established, and it has been determined that claims to the invention by several German pianoforte builders are false. Actually, Christoph Schröter had been experimenting with new actions in Germany as early as 1717 and was unaware of Cristofori and his activities. But Schröter did not get very far until 1725, when the design for Cristofori's action was republished in a Dresden journal. (The design had been published originally in 1711 in a Venetian journal.) The first German pianoforte builders, Schröter and Gottfried Silbermann, though they based their instruments on Cristofori's action, were responsible for the first distribution of the pianoforte, and the new instrument was thought to be a German rather than Italian innovation.

Cristofori probably built twenty pianofortes in his lifetime, of which two have survived. One, built in 1720, is in the Crosby Brown collection of the Metropolitan Museum in New York, and the other, built in 1726, is in Leipzig. Yet, Cristofori was not the first to think of the possibility of an instrument that was played by hammers. The phrase "piano e forte" occurs in documents of the Este family as early as 1598. We know of several instruments employing hammers that preceded Cristofori's, particularly that of Pantaleon Hebenstreit. This was a keyed dulcimer of five octaves, six feet long and played with hammers (like a xylophone) that was called the pantalon and which created a mild sensation at the court of Louis XIV at Versailles in 1705. Cristofori's pianoforte had four and a half octaves. It did not occur to him, apparently, to extend the range of his instrument beyond that of the human voice (from bass to soprano).

Though we know that Bach was exposed to the pianoforte in Germany and that Domenico Scarlatti may have known Cristofori in Florence and certainly became familiar with his instrument later in Spain, both men, like almost every musician of their time, were unaffected by it. Scarlatti was a harpsichordist, the last and probably greatest master of that instrument, rivaled only by Couperin as a performer upon it and by Couperin and Bach as a composer for it. We know little or nothing about how he played and where, since his performances were confined to small gatherings of the aristocracy in Italy, Portugal, and Spain, and only one unsatisfying account of his playing has survived in documents. But we know from studying his sonatas that he discovered in the harpsichord, just as its day was ending, subtleties and resources than even Bach did not suspect.

Scarlatti, whose father, Alessandro Scarlatti, was one of the most prolific and successful opera composers of the seventeenth century, left Italy at the age of thirty-three after working as an opera composer himself. He was fortunate enough to be freed from the life of a struggling musician trying to give the public what it wanted and was able to devote himself to his real interest, the harpsichord, through which his genius became manifest. In 1719, he became music master to the young Princess of Portugal, Maria Barbara, who later became Infanta and Queen of Spain. Scarlatti remained with her for the rest of his life and composed most of his 540 harpsichord sonatas either for her to play or for him to play for her. Certainly, Maria Barbara was an excellent player and must have performed most of the sonatas in private. It was Maria Barbara's stepmother-in-law, Isabel Farnese, second wife of King Philip V of Spain, who brought the first pianoforte to Spain. This was one built by Giovanni Ferrini after the Cristofori model. It was bequeathed to the great male soprano, Farinelli, the most famous singer of his time, who gave up his public career to serve, not only as a singer but as a political influence, at the Spanish court. When, after twenty-two years there, he was exiled by the new king, Carlos III, Isabel Farnese's son, Farinelli took this pianoforte back to Italy with him. Years later, the famous music historian, Dr. Charles Burney, to whom we owe much of what we know about musical life in the eighteenth century, interviewed Farinelli at his palace in Bologna and was shown the pianoforte that was one of Farinelli's proudest possessions.

Though Scarlatti did not invent the sonata form, he developed it extensively and used it with much charm and imagination. His harpsichord sonatas grew ever more subtle and beautiful. Strangely, they fell into obscurity after his death and were not generally appreciated until the beginning of this century, when they were published in an edition for the piano.

The word sonata (from *suonare*, to sound) originated about 1580 and originally indicated any piece that was played, as opposed to the cantata, which was any piece that was sung. The first harpsichord piece to be given the title sonata appears to have been composed about 1696 by Johann Kuhnau. The first sonatas to be published that were composed directly for the pianoforte appeared in 1732 and were the work of Lodovico Giustini. The strict sonata form, a development of the ascendency of the homophonic style over the polyphonic, was used loosely by Bach, Handel, and Scarlatti and finally was standardized by composers of the next generation, particularly Karl Philipp Emanuel Bach and Muzio Clementi. The strict sonata form applies only to the first movement, which should consist of three parts, exposition, development, and recapitulation, and should develop from two themes in contrasting keys.

The various schools of music that had evolved by the middle of the eighteenth century, when Bach, Handel, and Scarlatti died, still placed emphasis mainly on vocal music, though instrumental music had come a long way by that time. Since music in Europe got its impetus from Italy and traveled to Spain, Flanders, France, Germany, and England, it was appropriate that the pianoforte should be invented by an Italian but not surprising that Italians should have resisted it. Italy, being the seat of the Church and the country where singing was taken as seriously as life itself, always resisted change and suffered it badly, in the arts as in society. But even in the rest of Europe, musical traditions, once they were established, did not count for much until the nineteenth century. The general public, not knowing much about music but knowing what it liked, cared more for novelties than for the masterpieces of the past. Thus, the glorious music of Bach remained unknown to all but the most enlightened *connoisseur* for almost a century after it was composed. Even the music of Handel, so popular in England in its time, was regarded there for many years afterwards as suitable only for concerts during Lent, when it was considered unseemly to listen to music that people really enjoyed.

Johann Christian Bach

1735=1782

THE Bach family was the most musical in history. It produced professional musicians for eight generations, beginning with Hans Bach of Wechmar, who was born about
1520. In Germany for many years, any band of musicians
was apt to be known as "the Bachs," even though none of
them belonged to the family. This great musical line reached
its apex in the sixth generation, during the early eighteenth
century, when there were at least thirty Bachs in Germany
holding posts of importance in the musical world. Of these,
the greatest by far was Johann Sebastian Bach, whom many
believe to be the greatest composer who ever lived. From
1723 to his death in 1750, J. S. Bach was cantor of the
Thomasschule in Leipzig, which meant that he was required
to supervise the music of two of the city's leading churches
and for the university, as well as to oversee the musical
training and general education of the boys in the Thomasschule. His great cantatas were composed for special services of the Lutheran church-year and performed in the Leipzig churches. There are five complete cycles of these
amounting to some three hundred cantatas of which about
two hundred survive. The five Passions and the B Minor

Mass, as well as many other choral works, all were composed for church use in Leipzig.

➤J. S. Bach had twenty children, seven of whom died in infancy. Of his surviving sons—three by his first wife and two by his second—only one, Johann Gottfried Bernhard, who died at 24, failed to make his mark in music, though he did hold posts as an organist before turning to the law. The eldest son, Wilhelm Friedemann, was considered the most promising but came to a disappointing end. The second son, Karl Philipp Emanuel, was the most celebrated in his time and is the one best known to us now. However, the youngest son, Johann Christian, born at Leipzig on September 5, 1735, had a brilliant career that was completely outside the tradition of the Bach family. He was that which no other Bach ever was, a composer of Italian operas, and was the first of the Bachs to abandon the harpsichord and clavichord for the pianoforte, as well as the first musician ever to play a piano solo in public.

➤In 1736, Johann Sebastian Bach, the master composer for the harpsichord and clavichord, was exposed to the pianoforte, one of those built about 1730 by Gottfried Silbermann after the design by Bartolomeo Cristofori. Silbermann previously had been an organ builder and had constructed the instrument known as the pantalon for its inventor, Pantaleon Hebenstreit. This elaborate dulcimer-like instrument was one of the more interesting attempts to perfect an instrument struck with hammers that preceded Cristofori's successful pianoforte action. Silbermann tried to claim for himself the honor of inventing the pianoforte and succeeded, for many years before his death and afterwards, at least in Germany. History tells us that J. S. Bach was unimpressed by the pianoforte. However, his son, Karl Philipp Emanuel, who was to share with Muzio Clementi the distinction of perfecting the sonata form, became interested in the new instrument, though he did not actually adopt its use for another thirty-four years. The Silbermann pianofortes, like those of Cristofori, were shaped like harpsichords. About 1730, a pupil of Silbermann named Ernst Friederici built the first upright piano, which, in deference to the fashion for Greek names, he called the clari-cytherium. The first square piano, the type that for some time was to be the one most generally used, was built in 1742, probably by Friederici.

During the years that Johann Christian Bach was being trained by his father, the instrument on which he played was the clavichord. There is reason to believe that J. S. Bach was moved to complete his greatest keyboard work *The Well-Tempered Clavichord*, which he had begun twenty-two years before, in the year 1744 because of the extraordinary gifts of his youngest son, Johann Christian, who was then nine years old, the age at which J. S. Bach began the musical training of his children.

Johann Christian may have been distinctly different from his talented brothers because he was the son of a different mother. Anna Wülken, J. S. Bach's second wife, was a singer of great accomplishment and, as a descendent of the original Hans Bach of Wechmar, herself a member of the distinguished Bach clan. It is probable that Johann Christian was taught singing by his mother while his father supervised his practice at the clavichord.

It is interesting to speculate about what might have been Johann Christian's destiny if his father had lived long enough to complete his musical education. But, as it happened, the great Johann Sebastian died when his youngest son was fifteen. The family was left very badly off. Johann Christian inherited three claviers, a stock of linen shirts, and thirty-eight thalers (dollars). Anna Bach, who died ten years later, was forced to live as a charge of the city of Leipzig.

Since Karl Philipp Emanuel Bach, who was twenty-one years older than Johann Christian, held a good position as court musician to Frederick the Great in Berlin, it was logical that the boy should be put in his brother's care. Karl Philipp Emanuel dutifully sent for Johann Christian and accepted the responsibility of acting as his guardian and teacher.

It was at Berlin and Potsdam that Johann Christian was exposed to court life and the brilliant musical entertainments.

that Frederick the Great provided. Karl Philipp Emanuel's official position at court was that of cembalist (harpsichordist) to the Royal Capelle, which meant that he had to accompany the talented but tyrannical king through the three hundred flute concertos in his repertory. Some of these concertos were composed by Frederick himself.

The brightest jewel in Frederick's musical crown was his opera, which was the best outside Italy and upon which he expended a vast amount of money. He had built a new and luxurious opera house in Berlin in 1742. One of the eccentricities of Frederick's rule of his opera company was his stricture that all the operas performed, though composed in strict accordance with the Italian style, had to be written by German composers, while the singers must be Italian and nothing else. Admission to the performances was free and anyone could attend who was "decently dressed." The boxes were reserved for the nobility, but ordinary citizens had access to the pit. Frederick attended most of the performances and was fond of standing with the score before him on a music stand right behind the leader of the orchestra.

It was in this atmosphere that Johann Christian acquired his taste for opera. His brother drilled him methodically at the clavier and harpsichord; and during these years he began to compose. Most of his works from this period are clavier concertos. It is possible that he may have performed some of them at court, though there is no record of his having done so. It was also during this period that he developed his interest in the clarinet, the instrument for which he was one of the first to compose.

In 1753, Karl Philipp Emanuel published his treatise on clavier technique, which later masters, including Muzio Clementi and Johann Nepomuk Hummel, were to acknowledge as the chief source for their development of pianoforte technique. In later years, after he became city music director at Hamburg, Karl Philipp Emanuel's influence was to become very important in German music. Both Haydn and Mozart referred to him as "master."

It is not known exactly when or why Johann Christian left

Berlin and his brother's supervision, but modern historians agree that it must have been in 1756, when he was twenty-one. This was the year that marked the beginning of the Seven Years' War and the end of Frederick the Great's lavish productions in his opera house. Several theories have been put forward to explain how Johann Christian happened to go to Italy, some of them quite romantic but unsupported by facts. The most convincing theory is that he got the chance to go when someone was required to escort one of the prima donnas of the Berlin Opera back to her homeland. She had become seriously ill after the premiere of Graun's *Metrope,* the last important event in the fourteen years of Frederick's operatic patronage. It has been suggested that Frederick graciously made it possible for her to go home and for Johann Christian to escort her.

It must have been soon after Johann Christian's arrival in Italy, where he was without means, that he was fortunate enough to secure the patronage of the Chevalier Count Agostino Litta of Milan; and it must have been on the Count's behest that, sometime later, he went to Bologna to study with Giovanni Battista Martini, the musician-priest who later taught Mozart and was one of the most learned and respected teachers in Italy. Though he was enormously honored in his time and composed prolifically, we are familiar with Padre Martini today only through one song, the ever popular *Plaisir d'amour.*

Johann Christian also spent some time studying in Naples, where, after being converted to Catholicism, he began to compose liturgical music. It was his Mass, performed in Milan in 1758, that brought him his first real success as a composer. A *Te Deum,* performed soon afterwards, was equally successful. His duties as director of chamber music for the private chapel of Count Litta were not too demanding, and the count was very indulgent with his protégé. Even so, in 1760 he decided that Johann Christian would be better off if he were independent of him and, with this aim in mind, got him appointed to the important post of organist at

Milan cathedral. Thus, Johann Christian was provided with a modest income and the prestige of a good position. He was not required to play at all the services, having several assistants, but merely to supervise the music and maintain a certain standard. So, he was free to pursue his real interest, which was opera. This he did with a vengeance, for in the following year, 1761, two operas of his composition were produced with much success. The first, *Artaserse,* was given in Turin. The second opera, *Catone in Utica,* was produced at Naples and starred the soprano Catterina Gabrielli. She was known as "La Cochetta" because she was the daughter of a cook in the employ of Prince Gabrielli, whose name she adopted when her voice was discovered and he became her patron. She was one of the most admired and talked about singers in Europe and gained additional fame for her famous retort to the Empress Catherine of Russia. When the empress complained that she paid Gabrielli a higher fee than she paid her coachman, the soprano told her, "Then let your coachman sing for you."

The success of *Catone* in Naples was great enough so that Johann Christian composed another opera for the Teatro San Carlo there, which was produced in the following year, 1762. This was *Alessandro nell' Indie,* the last opera he was to compose in Italy. Pressure from Milan forced him to return to his post there in April, 1762. By this time, he had enjoyed sufficient success as an opera composer to be restless and dissatisfied in his safe but dull post as cathedral organist. So, when another chance came, he jumped at it, even though it meant leaving Italy forever.

The Princess Sophie Charlotte of Mecklenberg-Stielitz was a musical young lady who suddenly had been elevated from a provincial princess to Queen of England when she married George III in 1761. She wanted a new music master and requested her brother to find a suitable one for her. It was stipulated that he must be German and of sufficient fame to be worthy of the post that, until his death in 1759, had been held by George Frederick Handel, the Anglicized German who had been the most famous musician in England and one of the greatest composers of his time. Johann Christian's recent successes in Italy apparently had been noticed in Germany, for it was he the queen's brother recommended and to whom the offer was made. He set off for London by way of Germany in July of 1762. Except for three short excursions abroad, he was to spend the rest of his life in England and to become known throughout Europe as "the English Bach."

London for more than half a century had been one of the chief music centers of Europe and, it was known to all musicians, one of the best places to make money. From the beginning of the eighteenth century, the fashion there had been for Italian music, particularly for Italian opera and Italian singers. Handel had risen to glory on the wave of that fashion in 1711 and held on to his success until 1728, when the astonishing popularity of *The Beggar's Opera* created a new fashion for home-produced ballad operas. Handel had then recouped his fortunes by turning to the composition of his great oratorios, which appealed to the ever existing public taste for religious music. Strangely, the greatest era of English music, so far as composers are concerned, ended with the death of Henry Purcell in 1695. From then until modern times, the English passion for music had to be satisfied by foreign composers and, in the main, by foreign performers. Though every young lady of quality was expected to perform, however ineptly, upon the harpsichord, clavichord, or, in later years, the pianoforte, and many English gentlemen were accompished amateur musicians, the profession of music was not considered a respectable one during the eighteenth century and was suspect even during the nineteenth.

Public concerts became established in England somewhat earlier than in the other leading cities of Europe; and the first music publisher in England, John Playford, set up business as early as 1651. The first concerts to which anyone with the price (one shilling) would be admitted were given between 1672 and 1678 by John Banister, a violinist. The story goes that he had been expelled from the King's Band

and replaced by a French violinist. Feeling naturally disgruntled as well as in the need to make a living, he conceived the idea of advertising concerts in the London *Gazette* and giving them at his house, which he also used as a music school. He built a platform in the main room of his house and performed whatever was requested from the audience. The scheme seems to have worked well enough to keep him going and, after his death, these small concerts were continued, mostly in taverns. London's first real concert hall, Hickford's Room, was opened in James Street in 1713. It held no more than two hundred people.

Theaters, of course, had been flourishing in London, on and off, since Elizabethan times. The first real concert society, the Academy of Antient Music, was founded in 1710. This was a group that met in taverns and performed madrigals, motets, and anthems, with occasional performances by prominent soloists who came as guests.

The first pianofortes were imported to England about 1750. These were Silbermann and Friederici models. During the decade from 1750 to 1760, there was a vogue for novelties, such as the guitar, the lyrichord, musical glasses, performances in which the harp was played with one hand and the harpsichord with the other, and even a troupe of performing cats, which, it seems, were trained to howl on cue. Taste improved in the next decade, when a vogue for solo performances on the harpsichord began. Hitherto, that instrument and the clavichord generally had been regarded as suitable to accompany singers or to strengthen orchestras. In 1755, movable type was invented in Leipzig, Germany, which soon resulted in the mass distribution of printed music. This coincided with the arrival of the middle class as a buying power, fashion maker, and patron of the arts. About 1760, the first pianofortes were made in England by Roger Plenius and Johannes Zumpe; the latter was a pupil of Silbermann, who specialized in square models. The pianoforte was slowly gaining ground, though it did not win out over the clavichord and harpsichord until the end of the century. Still, as early as 1747, even before Johann Christian arrived at his court, Frederick the Great had as many as fifteen Silbermann pianofortes, from which we can deduce that Johann Christian, though he was familiar with it from an early age, did not take any real interest in the instrument until he was introduced to the Zumpe models in England.

In the London in which, in 1762, Johann Christian found himself, David Garrick, the king of actors, was appearing at Drury Lane; ballad operas were the rule at Covent Garden; and Italian opera held its own at the King's Theatre, Haymarket. The annual Lenten Concerts of sacred music, mostly by Handel, usually were given at Covent Garden. In the season, professional musicians, chiefly singers, performed in the highly popular public gardens where bandstands had been erected. Vauxhall and Ranelagh Gardens and the open-air theater at Sadler's Wells were now the places where young musicians tried their wings, seeking to attract the notice of the fashionable crowds that congregated there. By 1762, other musical societies had been formed, such as the Madrigal Society, made up mostly of church musicians; the Noblemen and Gentlemen's Catch Club, which met in the Thatched House Tavern in St. James Street; and the Society of Musicians of Great Britain, founded by the Corporation of the Sons of the Clergy in 1738.

Johann Christian was immediately successful in England. He was handsome, well educated, and apparently pleasing in society. We know very little about what he was like as a person, though it seems safe to conclude from what we know of his career that he got along well with people, especially fellow musicians, and was held in esteem by the royal family and their court. Subsequent to his death, biographers perpetuated a legend that Johann Christian was a drunkard and possessed of loose morals. They had no documentary evidence for this claim, and recent biographers have discovered evidence that indicates it was not Bach but his long-time partner, Karl Friedrich Abel, whose habits and morals were not of the best. The two men became confused and the wrong one, being the more famous in history, was forced to take the blame for about two hundred years.

Queen Charlotte, of whom the composer Haydn later said that she "played quite well, for a queen," allowed Johann Christian sufficient freedom so that he could pursue interests outside the court, though he went to Buckingham Palace several times a week, supervised the musical training of the royal children, and arranged and played at musical entertainments given at court.

The King's Theatre, designed by Sir John Vanbrugh, a celebrated architect and playwright, was opened in 1705. Though it had been the traditional home for Italian opera in London ever since, its fortunes were on the decline when Johann Christian went to work for it. The chief trouble came from a lack of good singers. Fortunately, Johann Christian's first production there, a pasticcio made up of numbers by various composers with an overture by himself, was a great success because it introduced a sensational new singer, Anna Lucia de Amicis. Three months later, on February 19, 1763, she starred in the first original work that Johann Christian composed in London, his opera *Orione*. The playbill states that the music was composed by Mr. Bach, a Saxon Professor. King George and Queen Charlotte attended the performance. The opera had several repetitions, and—a sure sign of success—a book of favorite arias from it was published almost at once. Since a collection of his harpsichord concertos, dedicated to the Queen, was published in the same year, it is evident that Johann Christian established himself in the London musical world both quickly and easily. It was a small world, however, in which competition was intense, fashions capricious, and fortunes extremely variable. Johann Christian's appointment at court, which he surely would not have held for so many years had his behavior been as notorious as later was claimed, safeguarded him against the perils of the professional music world. It is interesting to discover that in these times, musicians, despite their jealousies and rivalries, usually stuck together. The

June 2, 1768, the pianoforte made its world debut as a solo instrument at public concerts. This was at the Large Room, Thatched House, St. James Street, and the pianist was Johann Christian Bach. He probably played one of his own Sonatas, op. 5. From then on, Johann Christian used the pianoforte more often than the clavichord or harpsichord. The instrument that he played was a Zumpe square that he had bought for fifty pounds ($250). In the same year, the first solo performance on the pianoforte at the *Concert Spirituel* in Paris was given by a woman, Mlle. Lechantre. Two years later, Johann Christian's eminent brother, Karl Philipp Emanuel Bach, finally adopted the pianoforte as his instrument in Hamburg. Even so, the pianoforte did not become accepted generally at least until 1785.

We do not know much about Johann Christian as a pianist, but we do know that when he introduced a new pianoforte player at one of his own concerts on May 2, 1772, he produced a formidable rival to himself. This was Johann Samuel Schröter, who now is considered to have been the first master pianist to perform in London. He eventually succeeded Johann Christian as music master to Queen Charlotte.

During the last years of his life, Johann Christian suffered disappointments and financial setbacks. He made several attempts to duplicate Handel's feat of changing success in opera for that in oratorio. Though he composed only one more opera for London, he did go twice to Mannheim, then the most musical city in Germany, where two operas had been commissioned from him. These works, performed in 1772 and 1776, were considered successes, though they were in the old *opera seria* style that definitely was in the decline and which even Mozart was unable to revive successfully. It was to be Johann Christian's fate to suffer comparisons with the pioneers of opera as we know it, men of genius like Gluck and Mozart who also had theatrical instincts and were able to change opera from a ritual to a dramatic entertainment. However, Bach was unaware of this and was en-

couraged by his reception in Mannheim, where the opera
house seated five thousand people and was lighted by candles
that cost forty pounds a night to supply.

It was after his first trip to Mannheim, when he had been
refused in marriage by a young girl, that Johann Christian
married an old friend, the Italian soprano Cecilia Grassi,
who had made her London debut in one of his operas six or
seven years before. It is even possible that Johann Christian
had known Miss Grassi years before in Italy, when she was
still a child. She was a good singer, though she never enjoyed
much popular success. Her name went down in history,
however, because she sang Eurydice in the London premiere
of Gluck's *Orfeo ed Euridice*, the first work of his to be heard
there. Johann Christian revised and edited Gluck's masterpiece and gave it gratuitous additions of his own, thus bring-
ing upon himself the shame of having vandalized an opera
that was to become one of the oldest in the standard repertory of opera houses throughout the world. No doubt, Johann Christian was unaware of Gluck's revolutionary innovations and oblivious to their implications. Like so many
composers before and after him, he probably was merely
bewildered and hurt by the public's growing indifference to
his work and their interest in that of a newcomer. His final
opera, produced in Paris in 1779, was well received by the
French and temporarily revived his hopes. It was in Paris,
where he went to hear his opera, that he was reunited with
Mozart, who was now an adult and a master composer. Upon
his return to London, where he died three years later, Johann Christian devoted himself to his duties at court, where
his wife had become popular, and to the Bach-Abel concerts,
which continued until a few months before his death. But
even these concerts, which at the end were given in a new
and larger concert hall, the Hanover Square Rooms, declined
in popularity. Music was changing rapidly. Younger and
more brilliant performers had arrived in London, and
greater and more profound composers such as Haydn
and Mozart were beginning to be heard.

Though Johann Christian was only forty-seven when he died, he had been born early enough and lived long enough to be counted as a musician of the old school. History put him down as that and forgot about him. But in recent years, his music has been revived and found to be of surprisingly fine quality. We have today a different attitude toward music of the past. Knowing as we do how music progressed through many centuries, we judge it in its own context and enjoy it for itself without condemning one style because it does not conform to one that came after it. We are even becoming interested in the static *opera seria,* with the result that many forgotten works that preceded those of Gluck and Mozart are being revived. Johann Christian's opera, *Telemaco,* was produced by the Stuttgart Opera in 1965.

Johann Christian's contribution to the evolution of the piano and piano literature has been overlooked in favor of that of his brother, Karl Philipp Emanuel, who did more as a composer of pianoforte sonatas but less as a pioneer for the pianoforte as an instrument to be played in public.

It was inevitable that the sons of Johann Sebastian Bach should be overshadowed by him, though this did not happen during their lives, when their father was almost completely forgotten. Now that we have at last absorbed the great Bach in all his profundity and complexity, we can turn our attention to lesser matters, such as the real pleasure to be obtained from the music of his sons. When we look at Thomas Gainsborough's portrait of Johann Christian, which hangs in Bologna at the *Liceo Musicale,* where Johann Christian sent it as a gift to his old teacher, Padre Martini, we see a handsome man and remember that it was he who first did what so many have done since, which was to walk out on a concert platform, bow, and sit down to play the piano.

It was Mozart who said when he heard of Johann Christian's death that it was "a sad day for the world of music."

~3~

Muzio Clementi

1752 (?)-1832

ONE of the several mysteries about Muzio Clementi concerns the year of his birth. According to the records, he was eighty when he died. Yet his widow said he was eighty-two, and others said he was eighty-four. It may have been that his father, as the fathers of prodigies often do, concealed his exact age when he was a boy. So, in 1766, when all of Rome was talking about the Mass composed by young Clementi, which had just been performed with sensational success, he may have been fourteen, as people believed, or two or three years older. Five years earlier, the talented boy had attracted attention by winning the competition for the post of organist in one of the important Roman churches. Officially, he was nine at the time, though, more likely, he was eleven or twelve, since it seems hardly credible that a nine-year-old boy could defeat all the qualified adult organists who competed with him.

Clementi's father was a silversmith who was naturally musical. Recognizing unusual talent in his son, he started his training at a very early age, first with a choirmaster and then with an organist. Later, Clementi studied singing and counterpoint. The first Clementi composition to be publicly performed was an oratorio, given in Rome in 1764.

Perhaps the most important single event in Clementi's life

happened in 1766, when a member of a wealthy English family, Peter Beckford, M.P., came upon him in Rome. The evidence that Beckford actually adopted the boy for a sum of money is contained in a letter that, years later, Beckford wrote from Rome, in which he refers to: "the famous Clementi whom I found here in the year 1766 and bought of his father for seven years."

The seven years Clementi spent in the comfortable seclusion of an English country house in Wiltshire, England, were of great benefit to him. He was able, without undue pressure, to study and develop his gifts for composing and performing on keyboard instruments. We do not know exactly when he first played the pianoforte instead of the harpsichord; but it has been assumed that the wealthy Beckfords acquired one of the new instruments some time before Clementi left their custody in 1773, the year in which his first keyboard sonatas were published. His first appearances at London concerts, that year, were as a harpsichord player. He was immediately successful and soon was in demand as a teacher. It was not long before he was the most popular teacher in London. Eventually, he charged a guinea ($5.20) a lesson, a very large fee in those days, and a good part of the fortune he earned during his long life came from teaching those young ladies of the aristocracy whose parents believed that the more famous the player, the better he would be as a teacher. In Clementi's case, their faith was well placed for he was, apparently, as good at teaching as he was at playing and composing. And Beethoven acknowledged that his own piano technique was greatly influenced by a study of Clementi's early sonatas.

From 1777 to 1780, Clementi held the important post of cembalist of the Italian Opera at the King's Theatre. This meant that he played the harpsichord *continuo* and conducted the orchestra from the harpsichord. During this period, he must have been developing his pianoforte playing, for a year later he toured on the continent as a pianist, playing a new pianoforte built by John Broadwood. Broadwood,

who became the leading pianoforte builder in England,
began as a harpsichord maker in 1761. At first his pianofortes were modeled after the Zumpe squares; but, in 1780,
Broadwood began introducing improvements on which he
had been working for three years. He built the first grand
piano and developed the "English action" that was to become
standard for some years. This new action permitted greater
force but less speed. In 1783, after Clementi's first continen-
tal tour, Broadwood brought out a new grand with two foot
pedals, the loud or sustaining pedal and the soft pedal. Previously, the pedals, of which there were various types that
came and went as builders experimented with them, were
operated either like organ stops above the keyboard or as
levers operated by knee action below the keyboard.

Clementi's tour took him to Paris, Strasbourg, Munich,
and Vienna. He was received everywhere with acclaim and
was able to meet many famous musicians, including Haydn.
In Vienna, he was invited by the Emperor Joseph II to com-
pete as a pianist with Mozart, who was then twenty-five, four
years or more younger than Clementi. Mozart had adopted
the use of the pianoforte in 1777 and at the time of the competition had just entered into the ten-year period during
which he composed the seventeen magnificent pianoforte
concertos that he used for his performances in the salons of
the Viennese aristocracy. Mozart's piano at this time was one
built by Andreas Stein, who had learned his craft from a
nephew of Gottfried Silbermann, the first German pianoforte
maker. The vogue for the pianoforte in Vienna had gained
impetus in 1780 when the Countess Thun, an influential
aristocrat who was a musician and patron of music, acquired a Stein instrument that apparently was a great improvement on previous models. Mozart later used a pianoforte built by Anton Walter, which had a foot damper pedal.
Another Viennese pianoforte builder of this period was J.
Wenzel Schanz, whose model was that which was preferred
by Haydn.

Interesting details of the Clementi-Mozart contest have

come down to us. The two musicians performed before the
emperor and his court in the Hofburg, the palace of Vienna.
Clementi first played his Sonata in B flat, op. 47 no. 2, followed by an improvised toccata in which he exploited his
brilliant mastery of diatonic thirds and other double notes
for the right hand. Then, Mozart played a prelude and variations. After that, the emperor asked them both to read at
sight from some manuscripts of sonatas by Giovanni Paisiello. Mozart played the allegros and Clementi the andantes
and rondos. Finally, they played together at two pianos, ac-
companying one another as each improvised on themes from
the Paisiello sonatas. The emperor tactfully left the contest
undecided.

Afterwards, Mozart wrote in a letter that Clementi was:
"a mere mechanician, strong in runs of thirds, but without a
pennyworth of feeling or taste." Clementi, on the other hand,
was deeply impressed by Mozart's playing and, he later told
his pupils, was inspired to change his manner of playing.
Mozart's strength as a player was what was called his "singing" tone, which must have been derived from a skilled use
of legato, then very difficult to achieve on the pianoforte.
Perhaps his Stein instrument was superior to the Broadwood
instrument Clementi brought with him from London. At any
rate Clementi, when he returned to England, made a close
study of Italian singers and their legato techniques from
which, he must have known, Mozart had learned so much.
Certainly, the improvements Broadwood had perfected by
this time provided players with a better instrument; and the
six-octave grand that he introduced in 1794, too late to benefit Mozart, enabled the first real virtuoso pianists to emerge.

When Clementi returned to London, he had gained an international reputation. He did not leave England again for
twenty years for he was too busy performing, conducting,
and teaching. And, in addition, he went into business, becoming a partner in the firm of Longman & Broderip, "manufacturers of musical instruments and music-sellers to their
majesties." Perhaps Clementi's experience with Mozart in

Vienna inspired him to encourage his firm to build a new pianoforte, and he may even have made suggestions about its design. The pianoforte that Longman & Broderip offered for sale in 1789 was described as follows: "Soon as the hammer strikes the string it immediately falls back, whereas in other instruments, the hammer dances on the jack, and occasions jarring noise in the tone." This indicates as clearly as possible the problems presented by earlier pianofortes. The Stein piano on which Mozart played had no overtones, while Clementi's Broadwood did. Clementi may have decided that Mozart's beautiful legato effects were due, at least partially, to his instrument; and it may have been Clementi's zeal to improve his own playing that led, at least indirectly, to the new and improved Longman & Broderip instrument. As for the six-octave grand that Broadwood perfected and which was first played in public in 1794, various builders had been experimenting with it for some time. As early as the decade of the 1760's, a harpsichord maker named John Joseph Merlin had tried to combine the harpsichord with the pianoforte and in 1777 actually built a six-octave pianoforte for Dr. Charles Burney, who wanted an instrument wide enough so his daughters could play ducts at it and have room enough for their skirts and hoops.

Beginning in 1780, the concert programs in London regularly included pianoforte solos. But, whenever Clementi appeared, it was always in a concert in which his solos were interspersed by instrumental or vocal performances by other people. On March 10, 1784, the first two-piano performance on record was given by Clementi and his pupil Cramer at the Hanover Square Rooms. Concertos for two, three, and even four pianos with orchestra became popular later, in imitation of those composed for harpsichord and clavier earlier in the century.

That Clementi, unlike many artists, was a good businessman seems evident from his ultimate success as a music publisher and instrument maker. Though he suffered a severe setback in 1798 when Longman & Broderip failed, he quickly reorganized the company with John Longman as partner. Clementi became the sole proprietor in 1801, when the company became known as Clementi & Co. A disastrous warehouse fire in 1807 resulted in a loss to Clementi of 40,000 pounds. Still, he continued and eventually recouped. As a music publisher, he presented to England many works of Haydn, as well as the Fourth Symphony, Fourth Piano Concerto, and the Violin Concerto of Beethoven. He remained in charge of the company until 1830, when it became known as Collard & Collard.

Clementi went abroad again in 1802. He took with him as pupil and musical apprentice the young John Field, who later became famous in his own right. In Vienna, Clementi met Beethoven; and in Germany he gave lessons to a young man named Jakob Liebmann Beer who, as Giocomo Meyerbeer, was to become an international sensation when his opera, *Robert le Diable*, was produced at the Paris Opera (November 21, 1831).

On September 15, 1804, Clementi married a Miss Lehmann, daughter of the cantor of the famous Nikolaikirche in Berlin. She died in childbirth the following year, after a trip with Clementi to Italy. It may have been this loss that caused him to go to Russia instead of returning to England. He did very well in Russia, both as a performer and salesman for his own pianofortes. He returned to London in 1810 and married again the following year. This wife, too, he was to lose. He was middle-aged when he married a third time and became the father of several children.

After his return to London, Clementi gave up playing in public, though he never lost his skill as a player. Some of his pupils, particularly Moscheles, have left us accounts of their amazement at his powers of improvisation and powerful technique when he was over eighty. He was a man of enormous industry and many accomplishments. His *Introduction to the Art of Playing on the Pianoforte*, published by his own company in 1800, was the first work of its kind, the first "school," as such pedagogical works came to be known. The

only work of its kind for keyboard instruments that had preceded it was one for clavier written by K. P. E. Bach. Another
distinction came to Clementi on March 8, 1813, when he
conducted from the piano at the first concert of the Philharmonic Society in the Argyll Rooms, a new concert hall that
had been built in 1800 but had been used only for balls and
vaudevilles until then. The orchestra consisted of thirty
players. The Philharmonic Society, now the Royal Philharmonic, has been in continuous existence ever since and can
claim to have been one of the first of the world's major symphony societies.

Though the sonatas of Clementi have been known to almost every piano student and now are becoming recognized
as musically more important that most people thought, his
most famous work is his *Gradus ad Parnassum,* a group of
a hundred studies in pianoforte technique. The title (liter-
ally, "steps or levels toward Mount Parnassus") explains Clementi's intention, which was to develop excercises that
would bring a student's pianoforte technique gradually to
(or at least near to) perfection. Many a great pianist in the
years to come cut his virtuoso's teeth on this work.

As a composer, Clementi was surprisingly prolific, considering his business activities and his great amount of teaching. Of the twenty symphonies that he composed between
1786 and 1832, twelve of which were performed at London
concerts, only two have survived. Nobody knows what happened to those manuscripts, except that, after his death, a
family maid burned a great pile of his music, thinking it was
worthless paper. The sixty-four Clementi sonatas that have
survived are the works through which he developed the sonata to its final form. This work was begun by Scarlatti, continued by K. P. E. Bach, and finished by Clementi. Edward
Dannreuther, a well-known musician, once wrote that Clementi "may be regarded as the originator of the proper treat-
ment of the pianoforte as distinguished from the harpsichord." In recent years, musicians who have made profound
studies of the Clementi sonatas have been moved to make

surprising claims for them, such as that they contain many examples of musical prophecy, anticipating the technical and harmonic devices of Chopin, Schumann, Mendelssohn, Brahms, and even those of Debussy and Scriabin. Perhaps there is something in this and perhaps Debussy, at least, was aware of it when he composed his *Gradus ad Parnassum* in witty tribute to Clementi almost a hundred years after the original *Gradus* was published.

An ironic footnote to the famous Clementi-Mozart competition can be found in the fact that Mozart used a theme from the very sonata that Clementi played on that occasion in the overture to his opera, *The Magic Flute*. Perhaps this, too, was intended as a tribute. Certainly, Mozart had no need to borrow from anybody. And by that time, Mozart, who was in the last year of his life, may have realized Clementi's importance in the development of the pianoforte and the pianoforte sonata.

Clementi's long life began just as the lives of Scarlatti, J. S. Bach, and Handel were ending. He outlived Haydn, Mozart, Beethoven, and Schubert. In 1824, eight years before Clementi's death, the young Franz Liszt had created a sensation in London. In the year of Clementi's death, Frédéric Chopin established himself in Paris. The pianoforte had become a very different instrument from the one that Clementi first played in public. The use of iron to reinforce the sounding board, begun in 1820, made it possible for the famous virtuosos who evolved at this time, many of whom were Clementi's pupils, to play with a power and force never before possible.

So, it was appropriate, when Clementi died in 1832, that he was buried in the cloisters of Westminster Abbey and that on his tombstone it was written that he was called "the father of the pianoforte."

4

Jan Ladislav Dussek
1760=1812

UNLIKE Clementi, his near contemporary, Jan Ladislav Dussek, once a great name in music, has been all but forgotten. Students no longer play his sonatas and his compositions seldom if ever appear on concert programs. Yet, the same claims have been made for his sonatas that have been made for the far more familiar ones of Clementi; that is, in many ways they anticipate composers like Liszt, Schumann, Chopin, Brahms, and, particularly, Dvořák.

Dussek's life was a strange one. It began in a small town, Caslov, in Bohemia, which is now Czechoslovakia. Born on February 12, 1760, he was the son of an organist, Jan Josef Dussek. There were a good many musicians from Bohemia named Dussek, all related in some way. All three of Jan Josef's children had careers in music. Jan Ladislav, who was the oldest, started clavier lessons at five and organ lessons at nine. It is not known how early in life he began playing the pianoforte. However, it seems unlikely that one of the new instruments would have been available in a small Bohemian town as early as 1765. His first contact with the pianoforte could have been made when he was a student at the Jesuit College and organist of the Jesuit chruch in Kutuattora; but it seems more probable that he first encountered the instrument that was to become his in Prague, where he went to study theology.

Perhaps Dussek would have gone into the church rather than becoming a professional musician if he had not been discovered by a patron, Count Männer, who encouraged him in music and gave him the necessary security so that he could develop his talents fully. He was nineteen when the Count took him to Holland and Belgium (then a single country) and secured for him an organist's post at Bergen-op-Zoom. During the next three years, he began to compose and worked to develop his pianoforte technique. It was not until he was twenty-two that he first appeared at a public concert. This was at Amsterdam, and he created a furor. The result was not, as it would be today, a great many more concerts, but an opportunity to teach at The Hague. A year later, still displeased with himself as a player, he went to Hamburg to study with the city music director, Karl Philipp Emanuel Bach, a great clavier player who had mastered the pianoforte. Always restless, Dussek did not stay long in Hamburg but, the following year, went to Berlin, where he performed in concerts not only on the pianoforte but also on the harmonica, the instrument that had been invented in 1760 by Benjamin Franklin and improved by the addition of a keyboard about 1784. It is possible that Dussek was the first serious musician to play the improved harmonica in public. Both Mozart and Beethoven later composed music for it. This was not the harmonica that we know today, which commonly is called the mouth organ, but the glass harmonica, a collection of water glasses that produced tones by friction.

Dussek's wanderings next took him to Russia, where he spent a year at the court of Prince Radziwill in Lithuania. Then he traveled to Paris, where he played for the Queen, Marie Antoinette, and to Italy, where his performances were mostly on the harpsichord since the pianoforte, though it was invented there, was as yet hardly accepted. He returned to Paris in 1788 and remained for two years, teaching and performing. But the approach of the French Revolution was all too evident by then, and he decided to go to London, where he at once became Clementi's rival and for some years had no other equal except young J. B. Cramer, Clementi's pupil.

Though the honor was later claimed for Franz Liszt who was not yet born, Dussek appears to have been the first pianist to turn the pianoforte sideways instead of playing it either facing the audience or with his back to it. And, just as it was later said of Liszt, he supposedly made this radical innovation, which eventually was to become a permanent change, in order to display a handsome profile. In 1794 another Dussek "first" occurred in London when he gave the first public performance on the new Broadwood six-octave grand. This new pianoforte helped him to gain a reputation for the "singing tone" that Clementi had worked so hard to develop after hearing Mozart play ten years before. Clementi and Dussek both claimed to be creators of this "singing tone"; but it seems apparent that Dussek gained the advantage over Clementi when he adopted the use of the new Broadwood grand. Clementi, of course, was committed to the pianoforte that was developed by his own company.

Dussek, like Clementi, went into business in London, but, unlike Clementi, was not a good businessman. He went into partnership in a music shop and in 1792 married his partner's daughter, Sophia Giustina Corri. Mrs. Dussek was a talented singer, harpist, and pianist. She sang or played the harp at almost every Dussek concert in London and also composed pieces for the harp and pianoforte.

In 1800, the business of Corri and Dussek failed. Dussek was so much in debt that his creditors were threatening imprisonment. He was forced to flee. History does not reveal why Corri, too, was not in the same predicament. Perhaps Dussek had heavy personal debts as well as those affecting the business. Or, perhaps, he really wanted to go, or Mrs. Dussek and her father wanted him to. At any rate, Dussek left without his wife and never saw her again. Nor did he ever see the daughter that was born some months after his departure. This was Olivia Dussek, who was organist of

Kensington Parish Church and a composer of some accomplishment.

After leaving London in these unhappy circumstances, Dussek went to Hamburg, where he gave concerts, and then to Prague. While staying at Prague and performing there, he was able to visit his father, whom he had not seen in twenty-five years, at Caslov. In 1803, he secured what, apparently, he had always wanted, which was the patronage of a powerful prince who would relieve him of the obligation to teach, arrange his own concerts, and dabble in business. He wanted to compose; and the appointment at Magdeburg to Prince Louis Ferdinand of Prussia promised to provide the ideal conditions.

Prince Louis Ferdinand, a nephew of Frederick the Great, was even more musical than that formidable monarch. A fine amateur pianist and talented composer, he had been one of the earliest admirers of Beethoven, who was still a young man at this time. One of his compositions, the Rondo for piano and orchestra, is still performed today and has been recorded.

Unfortunately, Dussek's ideal existence at Magdeburg lasted only three years, for Prince Louis Ferdinand was killed at the battle of Saalfeld in 1806. The sorrowing Dussek composed one of his best works, the *Élégie harmonique*, op. 61, in memory of his patron soon after learning of his death. It is interesting to note that the vogue, soon to become widespread, for giving romantic titles or subtitles to piano compositions, was anticipated by Dussek, who gave to some of his sonatas such titles as *The Farewell*, *Retour à Paris*, and *La Consolation*.

After a brief and unhappy time in the service of another German Prince, that of Isenburg, Dussek found again his ideal patron, this time in Paris. This was Prince de Bénévent, the famous statesman Talleyrand, Napoleon's Grand Chamberlain, who later helped rescue his country from ignominy after Napoleon's defeat.

The last six years of Dussek's life were comparatively

happy and pleasant. Talleyrand made few demands upon him, provided him with a comfortable living, and left him free to compose. Dussek had a few pupils, gave a few concerts, and enjoyed considerable prestige. One of his compositions of this period, which undoubtedly was inspired by Napoleon's exploits, is his *Military* Concerto. Altogether, he composed some hundred works for the pianoforte, including twelve concertos, fifty-three sonatas, and twenty-seven sonatas for violin and pianoforte.

Dussek died at Saint Germain-en-Laye, near Paris, on March 20, 1812. His old rival, Clementi, to whom he dedicated his Sonata op. 44 (*The Farewell*), outlived him by twenty years. Yet he, like Dussek, belonged to a period that was essentially transitional, the period during which the pianoforte came of age. They were both men and musicians very much of their time, not, like Mozart and Beethoven, who were their contemporaries, immortals whose works were not merely of their time but for all time.

5

Johann Baptist Cramer

1771=1858

"GLORIOUS JOHN" was the nickname frequently given to J. B. Cramer, who was called by Beethoven "the only good pianist of his time." That judgment was hard on Dussek and Hummel, who were the only two possible rivals to Cramer at the time Beethoven was speaking. But Beethoven was known for his strong views, particularly about the pianoforte, for which he wrote music to which no performer and no instrument of his time could do justice. He was happiest with the pianoforte that the firm of John Broadwood & Sons sent to him from London in 1818, a six-and-a-half octave grand on which Beethoven composed his great last three sonatas. It had more power than previous models, and Beethoven, who was almost completely deaf, could pound it unmercifully in the attempt to hear what he was playing. Even so, this instrument, no more than any other of the time, could not begin to encompass the full range of Beethoven's music. This was proven in October, 1965, when a young pianist played a concert in New York on a reconstruction of the Broadwood pianoforte. The critics found this performance of historical interest but agreed that Beethoven's sonatas sounded muffled, restricted, and brittle compared to the way they sound when played on a modern concert grand.

J. B. Cramer came from a strong musical tradition and had distinguished musical antecedents. His grandfather, Jacob Cramer, was a violinist of the court at Mannheim, which in his day was musically the most advanced city in Germany. Under the direction of Johann Stamitz, the Mannheim court orchestra had developed a method of ensemble playing that became known as the "Mannheim School" and influenced musicians throughout Europe. Wilhelm Cramer, the father of "Glorious John," was also a violinist of Mannheim, where J. B. Cramer was born on February 24, 1771. A year later, Wilhelm Cramer moved his family to London, where he became leader of the King's Band. He also, in later years, was leader of the Italian Opera in London and, in 1784 and 1787, was leader of two famous Handel festivals given at Westminster Abbey. Leader, in this case, means not conductor but first violinist or concertmaster. At that time, there were no conductors such as we know today. The orchestra generally was cued and directed by the cembalist, and the leader (concertmaster) was an even more important player than he is now.

Thus it was natural that J. B. Cramer should grow up loving the music of Bach, Handel, and Mozart and that he should receive the best possible musical training as a matter of course. His first teacher was his father. But, when it became evident that his talent was not for the violin but for the keyboard instruments, he was sent to study with two pianists, one of whom was Johann Samuel Schröter, the first person after J. C. Bach to play the pianoforte at London concerts. Later, Cramer became the pupil of Muzio Clementi. He also studied counterpoint with K. F. Abel, who was J. C. Bach's long-time partner in their London concert series. Though he first performed in public at the age of ten, Cramer did not really begin his career as a touring virtuoso until he was seventeen. That career was to last for fifty-seven years. One of his appearances while he was still a pupil was at the age of thirteen when he performed with Clementi in the first public performance ever given of a duet for two pianofortes.

Cramer's career was similar to those of other successful performers of his day. He depended on teaching for his basic income, composed prolifically, played the music that he really loved in private, and in public played what was expected of him, including the inevitable improvisations. Nobody today expects a piano virtuoso to improvise in public, whether or not he has the ability. But during the later eighteenth century and the first half of the nineteenth, improvisation was part of the performer's stock in trade. We read in the memoirs of the pianist Ignaz Moscheles that he played a two-piano sonata by Cramer with him at a London concert in 1822 and, at Cramer's request, hastily composed a final movement for it himself. The result was a great success and was described by a critic as "an unrivalled treat, an unprecedented attraction." Moscheles, who at that time played the Clementi pianoforte, used a Broadwood at this concert, as did Cramer. Moscheles described the Broadwood as follows: "The strong metallic plates used by Broadwood in building his instruments, give a heaviness to the touch, but a fullness and vocal resonance to the tone, which are well adapted to Cramer's legato, and those fingers softly gliding from key to key; I, however, use Clementi's more supple mechanism for my repeating notes, skips, and full chords." Moscheles also wrote the following about Cramer: "His interpretation of Mozart, and his own Mozart-like compositions, are like breathings 'from the sweet south,' but nevertheless he shows no hostility to me and my bravura style. Cramer is exceedingly intellectual and entertaining; he has a sharp satiric vein and spares neither his own nor his neighbor's foibles. He is one of the most inveterate snuff-takers. While I, as a pianoforte player, cannot forgive him for disfiguring his aristocratic, long, thin fingers, with their beautifully shaped nails, by the use of it, and often clogging the action of the keys. Those thin, well-shaped fingers are best suited for legato playing; they glide along imperceptibly from one key to another, and whenever possible, avoid octave as well as staccato passages. Cramer sings on the pianoforte in such a manner that he almost transforms a Mozart andante into a vocal piece, but I must resent the liberty he takes in introducing his own and frequently trivial embellishments."

Moscheles also describes a London concert of 1833 at which Cramer played a Beethoven *Polonaise* at two pianos with Henri Herz, a player who had just become popular in the fashionable salons of Paris. Moscheles compares Herz to "a young, frisky colt" and Cramer to a "well-fed, cream-colored state-horse, harnessed on great occasions to the royal carriage." He also tells us that at the same concert, which was for Herz's benefit, Cramer performed Mozart's *Fantasia in F Minor* with Johann Nepomuk Hummel, who must have been his closest rival until Moscheles himself came along. From these memoirs of Moscheles we learn something about Cramer's brother, Franz, who, though not so brilliantly gifted as "Glorious John," had a distinguished career as leader of the Antient Concerts and the Philharmonic Society and was given the title of "Master of the King's Musik."

Though based in London for most of his life, Cramer also lived for periods of time in Paris and Munich. He taught and gave concerts in various cities on the continent. In 1824, he went into business, organizing Cramer & Co., a successful music-publishing firm. He retired from its active management in 1842 and from public performing in 1845. Though he composed many works, including seven pianoforte concertos and 105 sonatas, his reputation now rests entirely on his Piano School, published in 1810, which contains eighty-four remarkable *études* (one hundred in later editions), known as the school of velocity, and a collection called *Tutti Frutti,* which contains fingerings, comments, and additions to pieces by J. S. Bach, Corelli, Scarlatti, Couperin, Rameau, K.P.E. Bach, J. C. Bach, Haydn, Mozart, Beethoven, John Field, Dussek, and Cramer. Beethoven used Cramer's *études* as a means of commenting on his own sonatas and other piano works, giving his views on how they should be played through his comments. Thus, the Cramer *études* are still invaluable to pianists studying Beethoven.

Music historians generally describe Cramer as having been overshadowed by the older Clementi and the younger Hummel, as well as by Beethoven himself. But it is evident that he was a valuable player if for no other reason than that he preferred to be an interpreter rather than a display artist. He played the great keyboard works of J. S. Bach, which were all but unknown to his generation. In fact, Bach was an almost completely neglected composer from the time of his death in 1750 until Felix Mendelssohn's efforts brought him into popularity some seventy-five years later.

Another account of Cramer tells us that "as a player he had remarkable expressiveness, supported by great development of both hands equally and of each finger." Ernest Hutcheson in his *The Literature of the Piano* writes of Cramer: "In his studies he sought with considerable success to unite musical ideas with technical utility, paving the way to the complete fusion attained by Chopin and Liszt." He adds: "Cramer by tuition and performance played an honored role in the formation of piano style. Beethoven admired him greatly as a pianist, on one occasion declaring that 'all the others went for nothing.' . . . "

~6~

Johann Nepomuk Hummel

1778=1837

Recently, a radio station that features classical music made a survey to determine what were its listeners' favorite compositions. When the results were in, the name Hummel appeared on the list. This caused people to ask "Who is Hummel?" It was a reasonable question since Hummel's name was the only obscure one on the list, though, obviously, it had become a good deal less obscure since a recording of one of his piano concertos had been played by that radio station.

But Johann Nepomuk Hummel was anything but obscure in his own time. In his prime, he was considered the rival of Dussek and Cramer for the title of best pianist. Clementi had retired, and the great virtuosos of the next generation, such as Moscheles and Liszt, had not yet appeared. The only other serious contenders for the title in Hummel's time were Daniel Steibelt and Joseph Wölfl, both of whom were showy players but, apparently, inferior musicians. Wölfl had the doubtful distinction of having been judged the winner in a pianoforte contest with Beethoven.

Hummel was born on November 14, 1778, in the Hungarian city of Pozsony, which was also known as Presburg and is now the Czechoslovakian city of Bratislava. His father was conductor of the local theater orchestra and director of the Imperial School of Military Music. Young Hummel was expected to become a violinist but, when set to studying, showed no aptitude for it. His father then tried him at the pianoforte and at once discovered that it was his instrument.

In 1785, the Emperor decided to discontinue the Imperial School of Military Music. The Hummel family then moved to Vienna, where the father got another job as theater conductor, this time in a small theater in the suburbs run by Emmanuel Schikaneder, a singer, actor, manager, and playwright. Schikaneder was developing the *singspiel,* a kind of play with music comparable to the ballad operas that had been so successful in England. His great success came in 1791 when he produced Mozart's *Die Zauberflöte* (*The Magic Flute*), for which he wrote the libretto and in which he sang the role of Papageno, the bird man.

It was soon after the Hummels' arrival in Vienna that they became acquainted with Mozart, probably through Schikaneder. The young Hummel so impressed the great composer with his talent for the pianoforte that he not only became his pupil but went to live with him for two years in his house. And it was Mozart who sponsored his Dresden debut in 1787. Hummel was then nine years old. The following year, his father took him on a tour through Bohemia, Germany, Denmark, and Great Britain. Mozart died in 1791 at the age of thirty-five while the Hummels were in England.

Hummel was a great success as a prodigy in Great Britain, first in Edinburgh, where he remained for some time; then in London, where he first appeared in 1791 in a concert with J.B. Cramer at the Crown and Anchor Tavern. He and his father spent two years in London, during which time he studied with Clementi.

We do not know why Hummel returned to Vienna at the age of fifteen instead of remaining in England, as so many musicians of the time did. Perhaps he was more than usually ambitious as a composer and wanted to study with the best teachers, who were to be found in Vienna. And, no doubt, the Hummels were homesick after five years away from Vienna.

The first teacher that Hummel went to for training in composition was Johann Georg Albrechtsberger. Among Albrechtsberger's pupils was Beethoven, who was then twenty-three years old. Hummel and Beethoven became friends. After some years as an Albrechtsberger pupil, Hummel was advised by Haydn, the aging dean of composers, to concentrate on composing for the theater where, Haydn must have said, the money was to be made. So, Hummel went to study with Antonio Salieri, who was court-director of music to the Emperor and the leading conductor of Vienna, as well as the composer of popular operas and church music. Though Hummel studied diligently and subsequently produced two operas and eight operettas his real talent was not in that direction.

In 1803, Hummel went off on a tour to Russia, where he was very popular. In those days, the wealthy and glittering courts of St. Petersburg and Moscow offered great opportunities to musicians. The Russians had not then developed many good musicians of their own and, being almost entirely dependent on Western Europe for cultural influences, were eager for foreign artists to visit them. The situation was somewhat similar in England; and London was the rival to St. Petersburg in attracting visits from touring virtuosos. However, not so many artists were tempted to settle down in Russia as were to do so in England. Paris, usually the Mecca for musicians in search of a career, was at this time recovering from the ravages of the French Revolution, though it was soon restored to its old status as a center of fashion and artistic activity.

In 1804, Hummel had the honor of being appointed to the post of *Kapellmeister* to Prince Esterházy at Eisenstadt. Haydn had occupied this position for almost thirty years, and it was considered one of the best in Europe. Hummel remained at Eisenstadt for seven years, but finally was dismissed for neglect of his duties, which probably meant that he spent too much time in Vienna. It was at Eisenstadt in 1810 that Hummel produced Beethoven's Mass in C Major. Beethoven attended; unfortunately, this caused a break in their friendship because Beethoven took offense at something Hummel said. Both men were self-conscious, awkward, and sensitive. Hummel was a large man, while Beethoven was short. Whatever the reason for their misunderstanding, it was finally overcome seventeen years later when Hummel, swallowing his pride, went to see Beethoven several times during his last illness. We know from Beethoven's final letters how pleased he was at this reconciliation.

After his dismissal by Prince Esterházy, Hummel lived for five years in Vienna, teaching and playing at concerts. In 1813, he married an opera singer, Elisabeth Röckl. Their son, Karl, was later to become *Kapellmeister* at Ausburg and several other German cities.

Family obligations made it necessary for Hummel to seek another permanent post. By this time, he had a great reputation as composer, player, and teacher, so it was not surprising that in 1816 he was appointed *Kapellmeister* at Stuttgart and, in 1819, at Weimar. Both of these posts were important, as the princes in question were generous patrons of music. The duties of *Kapellmeister* involved composing for special occasions, conducting the court orchestra and sometimes the court opera, and supervising all the musical activities of the court. Hummel held these positions at a time when conducting was developing into a special art, and he seems to have become very interested in and adept at it. His duties at Weimar were flexible enough so that he could go off on concert tours, sometimes for prolonged periods. He returned to Russia, played in Paris in 1825, appeared again in Vienna, and made two trips to England, in 1830 and 1833. During his stay in England he not only played at concerts but appeared as a conductor of German opera, which had suddenly come into its own when Carl Maria von Weber's *Der Freischütz* was produced with sensational success in 1821.

At Weimar, Hummel was closely associated with the great poet, philosopher, and dramatist, Wolfgang von Goethe, who also enjoyed the patronage of the Duke of Weimar. Hummel often played at Goethe's house. The author of *Faust* and other works that were to fascinate musicians for years held strong views about music, though he once confessed that he wasn't sure he understood any of it at all. He particularly enjoyed Hummel's extemporizations at the pianoforte. Apparently, Hummel was a master of this kind of performance, as was Beethoven, who acknowledged him as a worthy rival in that respect. Hummel, who could create lovely melodies, was no match for Beethoven as a composer, however, and was content to compose conservatively in the manner of Mozart or Haydn. He produced an enormous number of works, including, in addition to many stage works and much choral music, a double concerto for pianoforte and violin, six pianoforte concertos, and much chamber music. His piano method, or school, published in 1828, is very elaborate and contains some 2,200 musical examples.

As a performer, Hummel was once described as follows: "His style as a player was that of the Vienna school, neat, finished and unimpassioned, but he had dignity and force." Ernest Hutcheson writes of Hummel: "He sensibly proposed to use the same fingering for recurring technical figures and to begin trills with the main note instead of the note above. Modern practice has accepted his rule of fingering with the addition that exceptions are no longer made when the thumb falls on a black key. Chopin seems in his teaching to have favored the (Hummel) concertos above those of Beethoven."

7

John Field

1782-1837

"THE Russian Field," as he was known, was, in fact, Irish.
Born in Dublin on July 26, 1782, he was the son, grandson,
and probably great-grandson of professional musicians. His
father and grandfather ran a music academy. Though they
kept up appearances in a respectable part of town, their
lives, like those of all musicians of the time who were only
averagely gifted, were a struggle. So, it is not surprising that
when John Field, who was named for his grandfather,
showed remarkable talent at an early age, his father and
grandfather seized upon him as their great hope. According
to legend, the boy was drilled so unmercifully and disci-
plined so severely, particularly by the elder John Field, that
he ran away from home but, because he was hungry, soon
was forced to return. There is no doubt that he was harshly
treated at home; but many boys were in those days, as
Charles Dickens later pointed out in his novels. The treat-
ment of resident choirboys in church schools was so cruel
that it eventually became a national scandal when the conditions were exposed through the diligent work of one woman,
Miss Maria Hackett, known as "the chorister's friend."

When he was nine, the young John Field was sent to study
with Tommaso Giordani, a singer, composer, and teacher
who then was the most influential teacher in Dublin. The

boy made his public debut not long afterwards, playing at a benefit concert. Giordani was attempting at this time to emulate the famous Paris *Concert Spirituel* and began to give a series that he called Spiritual Concerts at the Rotunda in Dublin. Since respectable people did not go to theaters during Lent, concerts were particularly popular during that period. When John Field first appeared at the Rotunda on March 24, 1792, he was advertised as being eight, though he was in fact ten. He performed a rondo of his own composition on themes by his teacher, Giordani. Later, he became something of a local sensation with his variations on an Irish Folk Song, *Go to the Devil and Shake Yourself*.

The following year Robert Field, John's father, had a change of fortune. He was invited to Bath, the fashionable English spa, to become leader of the orchestra there. The gay and glittering life of Bath must have made a strong impression on the eleven-year-old John Field. His strong interest in singing may have developed at this time, since the arbiter of all things musical at Bath was a once-famous singer, Venezio Rauzzini.

Robert Field stayed in Bath for only one season of concerts and then took his family to London, where he had been appointed leader (concertmaster) at the Haymarket Theatre. Young John soon had further opportunities to hear famous singers. He also must have heard the second series of concerts given in 1794 by the impresario J. P. Salomon at which Haydn conducted his own symphonies. We know that during this time Haydn heard John Field play and predicted a great future for him. Perhaps this was at a concert at which, in 1794, Field played a sonata by Clementi, who had by then become his teacher.

It was the custom in those days for boys to be apprenticed to a master of some trade, though musical apprentices were somewhat unusual, perhaps. We do not know whether it was Robert Field or Clementi himself who made the original suggestion; but when Field apprenticed his son to Clementi and paid him the large sum of a hundred guineas for the privi-

lege, he thought he was doing the best possible thing for the
boy. And it must have been done at some sacrifice, as it was
not that easy for Robert Field to put his hands on five hundred dollars. Clementi was the most famous musician in
London and the most successful teacher. He was a shrewd
businessman and had the reputation of being fond of money.
Though he has since often been accused of cruelty to John
Field, the charge is probably unjust, for Clementi, though he
worked the boy hard and kept him on short rations, treated
him with affection and was proud of his achievements,
which he did much to bring about.

Clementi, undoubtedly, had recognized a good thing in
John Field. The boy's great musical talent was interesting for
its own sake; but his ability to improvise and perform the
most difficult works at so young an age were to prove very
useful to Clementi. Field spent long hours demonstrating
Clementi pianofortes in unheated warehouses. At this time,
Clementi had three such warehouses, where his pianofortes
were stored and demonstrated for prospective buyers. Many
a society lady and gentleman must have been amazed, when
they came to buy a pianoforte, at the demonstrations given
them by an awkward Irish boy of twelve or thirteen. Field
did this work for long hours almost every day and it must
have been drudgery for him, though it also must have helped
to spread his name and attract audiences when he performed in concerts.

Though Clementi kept his part of the bargain by teaching
his pupil and occasionally presenting him at concerts, the
compositions of Field do not reveal much of the influence of
Clementi, who was a strict classicist. He appears to have
been much more influenced by the sonatas of J. L. Dussek,
Clementi's strongest rival at this time, who played in London
during these years. The more sensuous music of Dussek,
which was in advance of its time, must have found a deep
response in Field, who in character resembled Dussek more
than Clementi.

When he was nineteen, Field's first sonatas, dedicated to
Clementi, were published by Clementi & Co. On February 20,

1801, Field played his first concerto at a Covent Garden Lenten Concert, performing in the interval between performances of Mozart's *Requiem* and Handel's *L'Allegro and Il Penseroso*. By this time, he had become well known in London and, if he wished, could have made himself independent of Clementi. It might have been better for him if he had. But he remained with Clementi, still working at the warehouses and still on short rations, despite his growing fame. Perhaps he was content and did not want to make the break, or Clementi was too powerful and persuasive a personality. However it was, Clementi did promote his apprentice-pupil, included him at parties and other social events, and, in 1802, took him to Paris.

Ignaz Pleyel, with whom Clementi and Field stayed in Paris, was a composer and music seller who, in 1807, was to found the firm of Pleyel et Cie that was to make the best-known French pianofortes. He was an influential musician in the French capital, which then was beginning to emerge from the terror of the French Revolution. No doubt he arranged the concerts at which Field played with such enormous success, performing works of Handel and Clementi; but it was his playing of Bach fugues that made the deepest impression, since they, like all of Bach's music, were hardly familiar to audiences in those days.

The main purpose of Clementi's visit to the continent was to demonstrate his pianofortes and establish warehouses for them in various cities. So, Field's services as demonstrator still were required. He and Clementi moved on to Vienna, where the Paris successes were repeated, and then to Russia.

St. Petersburg, a beautiful city on the Baltic Sea, must have appealed to Field from the beginning, despite the hardships of the climate and the fact that he could speak no Russian or either of the secondary languages used by educated Russians, French and German. Perhaps it was not the appeal of the Czar's summer capital, but some crisis in his relations with Clementi that prompted him to make the break with his old master there in that distant land. Or it may have been that he believed the independence he had never had and was never really to achieve would be more possible in a foreign country. Whatever the reason, when Clementi left Russia after some months, having successfully established a sales force for his pianofortes, Field stayed behind.

One of the few firsthand descriptions we have of Field comes from this period when the celebrated violinist, composer, and conductor, Ludwig Spohr, visited Clementi at his St. Petersburg warehouse. Later, in his memoirs, Spohr described Field as "a pale, overgrown boy . . . clumsy, diffident, and clad in an Eaton suit that was much too small for him." But he adds that when Field began to play "all his *gaucheries* were ignored and the real artist displayed."

Not long after Clementi left Russia in July, 1803, Field began to play at concerts and private parties and to acquire well-paying pupils. His independence was firmly established. But it must have come too late, for he also established at this time his bad drinking habits, which he was never to overcome. There is no doubt that he was weak, lazy, dissolute, and that he wasted a great talent. Being so gifted, it was easy for him to get by with the minimum effort, and the flattery of adulation from public and pupils, now that he was free of Clementi, who was a hardheaded realist and stern taskmaster, may have gone to his head. The simplest explanation of his shortcomings is that, subjected as he was for so long to strong authority, he was unable to mature fully when at last he was on his own. Still, it is surprising that Field, considering his weaknesses, accomplished as much as he did and was, in his way, faithful to his art to the end. It has been said that no other composer except the later Russian, Alexander Borodin, "laid claim to immortality with so small a body of work." Field's output was even smaller than Borodin's and on a smaller scale; but the music that he did produce has its own unique quality that sets it apart from the voluminous output of most of his contemporaries. Field's *Nocturnes* are still played and listened to today, while most of Clementi's music and almost all of Dussek's, Cramer's, Hummel's, and Moscheles' is not.

Field did not leave Russia for thirty years. Clementi returned in 1806 and found his pupil well established as a
player and teacher. In three years he had learned Russian,
French, and German. Clementi brought with him a pianoforte which he gave to Field in exchange for the publication
rights to several of his compositions. It is to be hoped that,
during this visit, Clementi did not become aware of his old
pupil's intemperate habits, which probably were not at this
time as strong as they were to become later. Though Field
was to become known as a "Bohemian" to the Russians, there
was more tolerance for that kind of life in Russia than else-
where, which may have been why he was content to stay
there. Russians, then as now, were not intolerant of drinking
but only of drunkenness. Field, it seems, was one of those
unfortunates who can tolerate his own weakness for drinking but can not tolerate alcohol. His emotional life, too, was
unfortunate. His love affairs did not turn out happily, and
his marriage, to an actress named Mlle. Percheron, which
took place in 1808, was not a success. However, she appeared with him at concerts, giving dramatic recitations, until their separation in 1813.

In 1814, Field published his first *Nocturnes*. He was now
at the height of his fame in Russia and was in constant demand as a teacher and performer. He suffered a major disappointment in this year when he was not, as he had reason
to think he might be, appointed to the important and lucra-
tive post of official pianist to the Czar. No doubt, his reputation for "Bohemianism" had something to do with this. The
man appointed instead was Daniel Steibelt, a German virtuoso, who also became conductor of the court opera in St. Petersburg. He and Field became friends and Field emulated
him in some ways, particularly in composing his fifth piano
concerto in imitation of Steibelt's successful *Grand Military
Concerto* for piano and two orchestras *In the Greek Style* and
of his concerto *Le voyage à Mont Bernard*. Field called his
concerto *L'Incendie par l'orage*. It was a great success.

Field's most famous pupil came to him in 1818 and received lessons from him, off and on, for four years. This was Michael Glinka, the man who was to become the first great Russian composer and the founder of the nationalist school of opera. Glinka left us an account of Field's playing in which he says that it was "at once sweet and strong and characterized by admirable precision. His fingers fell on the keys as large drops of rain that spread themselves like iridescent pearls."

Field moved to Moscow in 1822, probably on the advice of Steibelt. There, he acquired more pupils and continued to play at concerts and at the private entertainments given by the aristocracy and wealthy bourgeoisie. By this time, apparently, his weaknesses were well known and his death was reported in the newspapers twice in three years. He was forced to take advertisements denying the reports, thereby anticipating by a good many years the famous incident in which Mark Twain had to announce that "the reports of my death are greatly exaggerated."

In Moscow, Field became the teacher of an already famous woman pianist, Maria Szymanowska, with whom the great poet Goethe fell in love. Mme. Szymanowska made a place in musical history by breaking with the custom of performing a work of the pianist's own composition as the feature of a concert, giving instead whole programs of works by the great but mostly neglected composers for the piano. This was done not because she was not herself a composer, for she was, but out of love for Mozart and Beethoven. Another associate of Field's in Moscow was the famous pianist J. P. Hummel, the highly respected *Kapellmeister* of Weimar, a friend of Goethe and Mme. Szymanowska, who gave a Russian tour in 1822.

Field might never have become truly celebrated except for the fact that after thirty years of relative obscurity in Russia, he ended his life in a blaze of international glory. The impetus to leave Russia and attempt a tour came from an invitation to perform with the Philharmonic Society of London. The concert took place in February, 1832. Field played his E flat concerto to tremendous acclaim. He at once became one of the musical lions of London and was invited everywhere. The pianist Moscheles, who wrote a book of memoirs, to which we owe much of what we know of the musical personalities of this period, had the following to say about Field: "His legato playing delights me, but his compositions are not at all to my taste; nothing can afford a more glaring contrast than a Field *Nocturne* and a Field's manners, which are often of the cynical order. There was such a commotion yesterday among the ladies, when at a party he drew from his pocket a miniature portrait of his wife, and loudly proclaimed the fact that she had been his pupil, and that he had only married her because she never paid for her lessons, and he knew she never would. He also bragged of going to sleep while giving lessons to the ladies of St. Petersburg, adding that they would often rouse him with the question, 'What does one pay twenty roubles an hour for, if you go to sleep?' He played to us a good deal in the evening; the delicacy and elegance, as well as the beauty of his touch, are admirable, but he lacks spirit and accent, as well as light and shade, and has no depth of feeling."

A much more favorable impression of Field as composer and player was gained at this time by Moscheles' friend, the young composer Felix Mendelssohn, who was to call the world's attention to so much neglected great music.

It was ironic and probably appropriate that Field should have arrived in England just a few weeks before the death of Clementi. We do not know if he visited his old master on his deathbed or even if Clementi was aware of his pupil's sudden fame in England after the Philharmonic concert. But we do know that Field was a chief mourner at Clementi's funeral at Westminster Abbey on March 29, 1832. Two days later, he played with Moscheles and another Clementi pupil, J. B. Cramer, at a concert to celebrate the centennary of the birth of Haydn. It must have been soon after this that Field met Mendelssohn at Moscheles' house. Also in this year, Moscheles discovered that the life of a touring virtuoso was to be greatly aided by the new means of transportation, the railroad. Unfortunately, Field did not live long enough to benefit from this great new innovation.

When in June, 1832, Field went to Paris, it was to experience even greater triumphs than he had in London. He played at the Salle du Conservatoire and in a concert hall recently opened by J. H. Pape, who was now the rival to Pleyel as the leading pianoforte builder of Paris and who was experimenting with all sorts of innovations. Pape built pianofortes of strange shapes and sizes, some of them disguised as desks or cabinets, though it was not he who later was responsible for the pianoforte that converted into a bed. He also experimented with down-striking hammers, with an eight-octave piano, with overstringing, better felt hammers, and other improvements, some of which eventually became standard.

During this Paris visit, Field met the young Frédéric Chopin and heard him play. His description of Chopin as "a sickroom talent" afterwards became famous and, regrettably, was taken seriously by some as a just description of Chopin's pianism, which was delicate and refined to a degree but beautiful nonetheless. Field's influence on Chopin, particularly through his *Nocturnes*, the form of which the latter adopted, is well known. Both men were of a somewhat morbid turn of mind. It has been said that Field invented the *Nocturne* and poured his best efforts into it because everything about night appealed to him, that he was himself a "night person." This may have been why Chopin was so attracted to the *Nocturne* and why Field's harmonies made such an impression on him, though, more likely, he simply admired the music and liked the novelty of the *Nocturne* form.

Field next went on a prolonged tour through Belgium, Switzerland, Italy, and French provincial cities. In Marseilles, he was called by a critic "The Racine of the piano," a not inconsiderable compliment, since the playwright Racine was (and still is) one of France's national heroes.

This last tour of Field's occurred at a time when the public taste in piano music was somewhat better than it had been and was about to become. Already, the enormous success of Meyerbeer's *Robert le Diable* at the Paris Opéra, just a few months before Field's Paris visit, was having its effect. Soon, the public would be clamoring for piano fantasies on themes from that opera and others that were to come. For some years, pianists and piano music were to be dominated by the rage for opera. Meyerbeer, Donizetti, Rossini, Bellini, Weber, and, later, Verdi, were to compose the tunes that everybody wanted to hear, if not in the opera house, where they belonged, then in the concert hall. Not that Field, if he had lived, would have minded so much, since he loved and admired singing and composed some of his *Nocturnes* in imitation of dramatic vocal scenes, complete with introduction, arioso, recitative, and coloratura. Chopin, too, was much influenced by vocal music, particularly those superb subtle melodies in the operas of Vincenzo Bellini.

Field went from one triumph to another on his tour and, exhausted from all this unaccustomed work, attention, and excitement, arrived in Naples a very sick man. It was said that his illness was brought on by alcoholism. He was in a Naples hospital for many months. All his earnings from the tour were spent, he was unknown and neglected there, and pride would not permit him to appeal to friends in Russia for help. Suddenly, the man who so recently had been the rage was reduced to poverty in a strange city. Fortunately, soon after his release from hospital, his plight was discovered by a Russian family visiting in Naples. They took Field to the island of Ischia for a rest cure and then persuaded him to start home to Russia. The pianist's health was improved, for in Vienna, where he stayed in the house of Karl Czerny, the celebrated teacher, he was able to give three concerts. But not long after his return to Moscow, he fell ill again. After two months, during which he was faithfully attended by friends, he died, on January 11, 1837. The last of the several stories about Field, which may or may not be true, is that at his deathbed he was asked if he did not want spiritual comfort. First, he was asked if he was a Catholic, then, if he was a Protestant. When he still did not reply, he was asked, "Are you a Calvinist?" Field, suddenly rousing, answered, "No, no, I'm a pianist."

It was during Field's last illness, in November, 1836, that his pupil, Michael Glinka, began the great era of Russian nationalism in music with the production of his opera, *A Life for the Czar*, in St. Petersburg. John Field was a minor but nevertheless pronounced influence on Russian music, through his pupils and, particularly, his *Nocturnes*. It has been said that the Irish resemble the Russians, and there may be something to it, for Field must have felt at home in Russia or he would never have stayed so long. Like Shakespeare's Falstaff, to whom he once was compared by a contemporary, he was, though given much to wine and bragging, hard not to like if not to admire.

Though Field composed seven piano concertos and various other pieces, he is known today only for his *Nocturnes*, of which he composed seventeen. At least five of these were arranged as *Nocturnes* from movements of other works. Franz Liszt described the *Nocturnes* as *poésies intimes*, and also as "rose-scented." He had heard Field play in Paris and said that his playing was "too sleepy" for him, which was not surprising from the man who was one of the stormiest of virtuosos. However, Liszt thought enough of the Field *Nocturnes* to prepare and edit an edition of them. Robert Schumann was so impressed by the Seventh *Nocturne* that he helped spread its fame by writing an almost ecstatic description of it in his Leipzig music magazine.

François Joseph Fétis, the author of an important music history, had this to say about Field after one of his Paris concerts in 1832: "Whoever has not heard this great pianist can form no idea of the marvellous mechanism of his fingers—mechanism such that the greatest difficulties seemed to be the simplest things, and that his hands do not appear to move. He is not less astonishing in the art of attack, and of producing an infinite variety of *nuances*, whether as regards breadth, sweetness, or accent. An enthusiasm impossible to describe, a veritable delirium was manifested by the vast audience."

So far as Field's influence upon Chopin and the comparison between them is concerned, this is what a great authority, Edward Dannreuther, wrote in 1906: "The form of Chopin's weird *Nocturnes*, the kind of emotion embodied therein, the type of melody and its graceful embellishments, the peculiar waving accompaniments in widespread chords, with their vaguely prolonged sound resting on the pedals— *all this and more* we owe to Field!"

8

Karl Czerny

1791=1857

MANY weary students have cursed Karl Czerny, and even the most diligent and determined of them must at times have wished that this man had never existed. And yet, if Czerny had not existed, it is possible that the kind of piano virtuosity we know today might not have existed either.

Strangely, Czerny, who was a brilliant piano prodigy, never played in public as an adult. Instead, he became a prodigious music machine, a recluse who dedicated himself to teaching the most talented players of his time and composing so much music that his opus numbers extend almost to a thousand. The most famous story about him, which, though it may not be true, has always persisted, is that he always composed four pieces at a time in a room that had four music stands. When the ink was drying on the page on one stand, he worked at another, moving on to the next when he reached the bottom of the page. He worked incessantly all his life, and his friends all said when he died that it was overwork that had killed him.

Czerny, too, was the son of a musical father, who was his first teacher. The Czernys were well-to-do and fond of entertaining prominent musicians in their house in Vienna, where Karl Czerny was born on February 20, 1791. One of the musicians with whom the Czernys were intimate was

Wenzel Krumpholtz, a violinist of the Vienna Court Opera who was a friend and associate of Beethoven. He realized that the boy Karl had exceptional talent and, in 1800, when he was ten, took him to Beethoven. For the next three years, Karl Czerny was Beethoven's pupil, and was able to make a close study of the master's music and methods. It was said that Beethoven was so taken with the boy's talent that he used to put the piano sonatas he had just finished composing before Czerny and ask him to play them at sight. Later, Beethoven interested his patron, Prince Lichnowsky, in Karl; and before long, the gifted boy was the talk of the Vienna musical world. He became a pupil of Hummel and studied with Clementi when that master was on a visit to Vienna. He was fourteen when he produced his first composition, a set of variations for pianoforte and violin on a theme by Wenzel Krumpholtz that was published by a Viennese firm. The next year he was about to set out on a European tour, but he did not go. Political unrest, the result of the Napoleonic conquests, was given as the reason; but, since Czerny never again played in public, it must be assumed that that was an excuse. Perhaps Czerny had a deep-seated aversion to public performing, which, since his parents were prosperous, he could afford to indulge. Certainly, he could not be accused of laziness or apathy, since the rest of his life was given over to unremitting toil.

It was not long before Czerny, beginning when he was only sixteen, was so famous as a teacher that he was deluged with would-be pupils. However, he took only the most gifted or most advanced. His parents gave recitals for his pupils every Sunday in their house. These were attended by Beethoven and other famous musicians of the time.

About the year 1815, the pianoforte had become so strongly established in the musical world of Vienna that everybody wanted to study it, and the demand for pianists, piano music, and piano teachers appeared to be insatiable. The Stein pianoforte manufacturers, who had produced 1152 pianofortes in twenty years, was now divided in two.

One firm was managed by the original Stein's daughter and her husband, and the other by her brother. There were several rival pianoforte builders, such as Moser, Müller, Graf, Broadmann, as well as those in other countries who exported pianofortes to Vienna, particularly the Paris firm of Érard Frères, established in 1802. In 1828, Ignaz Bösendorfer established his firm, which was destined to become the most successful in Vienna. Another phenomenon of the time was the emergence of first-rate women pianists, of which the two most important were Marie Bigot de Morogues and Dorothea von Ertmann, both of whom were among the first to perform Beethoven's late sonatas. The *Sonata in A,* op. 101 was dedicated to Mme. von Ertmann.

The time was right for a Czerny. His was the authority that everybody accepted, though few ever heard him play. His genius was for the technical aspects of pianism; apparently he was obsessed by them. Perhaps his years with Beethoven, during which he got into the habit of copy editing, proofreading, and transcribing for the master, gave him a taste for this kind of activity. All during his life, arrangements and transcriptions of other people's works poured forth from his studio to meet the demand for anything and everything that could be played on the pianoforte. There were times when he had as many as twelve pupils a day, each of which he drilled in the exercises he slowly was devising, which were to become familiar to students all over the world. He was reputed to have had a sour disposition; and a lesson with him must have involved little if any nonsense. There is a legend that Beethoven "despised" Czerny's "free" style of playing because it had no legato; but if that was the case, it seems strange that he would have sent his beloved nephew, Karl Beethoven, who was to cause his uncle so much anguish and disappointment, to Czerny as a pupil.

In addition to all his transcriptions and original compositions, Czerny published during his life treatises on finger dexterity, velocity, studies in legato and staccato, improvisation, fugue playing, and composition. His gigantic *Complete*

Theoretical and Practical Pianoforte School, published in 1839, contains all this and much more, even including advice on how to choose, tune, and re-string a pianoforte. His op. 822 was a new *Gradus ad Parnassum,* intended to bring that of Clementi up to date. His op. 500, which was part of his complete piano school, was dedicated to Queen Victoria of England. The fruits of his huge labors also included an autobiography, editions of Bach's keyboard works, and of two hundred of the Scarlatti sonatas.

Czerny's fame was very great in his own time; and it was said that he knew everybody who was anybody in the musical world of Europe. Yet he hardly ever left his house; the world came to him. So reluctant was he to leave his work and familiar environment that he made but three short trips away from Vienna during his life, visiting Italy, Paris, and London, where he was received with a respect and deference denied to most musicians.

To us today, Czerny's name is exclusively associated with his *études,* which must be the best and most complete piano excercises ever composed. Some critics have even claimed that they are the equal in musical quality to those of Chopin, which were not composed as exercises. Certainly it is true that if one has the rare opportunity of hearing a Czerny *étude* played as music and not as a duty, one can be struck by how good it is, for Czerny could compose with charm and sometimes with power. And one wonders what all those Masses, Requiems, symphonies, overtures, concertos, trios, quartets, and choruses he composed are like. Since they remain in manuscript and have never been published and it does not seem likely that any of them will be performed again, one has to take posterity's word for it that they are worthless. Perhaps Czerny suspected that his more ambitious compositions would not survive him, for he left part of his fortune as a fund to provide for performances of his liturgical works. It is interesting that the rest of his money was left to a school for deaf mutes.

Theodor Leschetizky, who became the most famous of all

piano teachers and whose pupils were the teachers of some of today's great pianists, always claimed that he had no methods, no secrets, no knowledge except those of his teacher, who was Karl Czerny.

~9~

Ignaz Moscheles

1794=1870

IGNAZ Moscheles lived during one of music's greatest periods. When he was young, he knew Beethoven. In his old age, he met Wagner and was aware of the tremendous influence he was to have. Though Moscheles was the friend and often a respected associate of Weber, Mendelssohn, Rossini, Schumann, Berlioz, Chopin, and Liszt, he was not destined to share in the permanent glory that belongs to all of them. If musicians and music lovers speak the name of Moscheles today, it is only in connection with the cadenzas he composed for the Beethoven concertos, which still are performed occasionally. Yet, he was in his time a very important musician, much admired as a pianist to the end of his life, and held in the highest esteem by his contemporaries. In later years, he liked to refer to himself as the link between the old and modern schools of piano playing. Firmly grounded in the tradition of Clementi, he found himself overshadowed by younger and stronger virtuosos such as Franz Liszt and Sigismund Thalberg. But he held his own and maintained his following throughout a career that kept him before the public for more than fifty years. He did not much care for being called "old-fashioned," as he was to be in his old age, but he bore it with the calmness and philosophy that were characteristic of him.

Prague, where Moscheles was born on May 30, 1794, has always been a city of musicians. Moscheles' father, a cloth maker, was a good amateur guitarist and singer. He soon recognized his son's unusual talent and sent him, at the age of seven, to the director of the Prague Conservatory, Dionys Weber. Weber took him as a pupil with the provision that he give up his childish infatuation with the music of Beethoven, who, Weber said, "clever as he is, writes a lot of harebrained stuff, and leads pupils astray." The regimen set by Weber for the young Moscheles was that he was to play nothing but Mozart the first year, Clementi the second, and Bach the third. Old Weber may have been a musical reactionary, but he must have been a good teacher, for by the time Moscheles was fourteen, when the sudden death of his father made it necessary for him to earn his own living, he was able to do so. A few weeks later, he made his first professional appearance at a private musical party arranged by Weber, playing his own first pianoforte concerto. Then, he was sent off alone to Vienna to make his way.

The music publisher Domenico Artaria, with whom, a few years earlier, Clementi and John Field had stayed while en route to Russia, was Moscheles' first patron in Vienna. Artaria helped him get odd musical jobs, such as copying and arranging, and sent him to study with J. G. Albrechtsberger, one of Beethoven's teachers. Soon Moscheles made the acquaintance of Beethoven, who was then almost forty. The great composer was impressed with the young teen-ager and gave him the important commission of arranging the piano version of his opera, *Fidelio*. Before long, Moscheles was gaining a reputation and began to get engagements playing at private parties and, occasionally, concerts. He became friendly with the pianist Hummel, the future opera composer Meyerbeer, and the violinist Ignaz Schuppanzigh, who was leader of the famous Razoumowsky Quartet, which first performed many of Beethoven's chamber works. After Moscheles became a pupil of Antonio Salieri, the old enemy of Mozart who was the occupant of most of the important

official musical posts in Vienna, he was made Salieri's dep-
uty *Kapellmeister* at the court opera.

The year 1814 was an important one for Europe and for
Moscheles as well. The glittering Congress of Vienna, held to
determine the fate of nations after Napoleon's first defeat,
was the occasion for gala concerts and balls. Many emper-
ors, kings, and princes were in the city. Moscheles was commissioned to compose some music for a great fête given in
the beautiful Spanish Riding School connected with the Hofburg, or Imperial palace, of Vienna. This led to more commis-
sions, and he rapidly composed such occasional pieces as
The Entry Into Paris and *The Return of the Kaiser,* as well as
a cantata commissioned by the Jewish Congregation of Vienna. All this resulted in a great demand for his services as a
teacher, and he soon had more pupils than he could handle,
though he was still only twenty years old. He began to play
in public more often and was soon being talked about as
Hummel's rival, which attracted large audiences when the
two pianists performed together.

The first great success that Moscheles enjoyed came when
he played a new composition of his own at the *Kärtnertor-
theater* on February 9, 1814. This was a set of variations for
piano and orchestra, on the march played by the regiment
that bore the name of the Czar of Russia. These *Alexander
Variations* were to become Moscheles' warhorse, gaining
popularity all over Europe, and he was to perform them
again and again for many years. There was a vogue for this
kind of composition.

In 1816, Moscheles left Vienna to seek greater fame else-
where. He lived for some time first in Leipzig, then in Dresden, where he had the experience of performing for the court
while it was at dinner. It was at Dresden that he carefully
studied the social and professional customs of the time, so
that he was able to make his way easily both among musicians and among the nobility, on whose good will and patronage a career in music depended. He set up the pattern
that he was to follow for some years, winning a following in

one city and then, armed with letters of introduction, going off to another. He learned well how to make contacts and use them. But he was a pleasant, well-mannered man; practical, industrious, and enormously accomplished, he made friends easily. To his credit, he always kept his friends and once said that the only way to deal with enemies was to force them to become friends. His was the good fortune to achieve success early and, through hard work, resourcefulness, and good sense, to keep it. Perhaps his one great fault was lack of imagination, which caused his own music to fall into obscurity and made it difficult for him to understand the music of younger composers such as Berlioz, Chopin, Liszt, Schumann, and Wagner. He was always careful to look for things to admire in new music but, it is evident in his memoirs, often failed to comprehend the purpose and importance of innovations.

After some time in Paris, where he chose the Pape piano in preference to the Érard, Moscheles settled in London, and made his debut on June 11, 1821, with the Philharmonic Society, playing his *Alexander Variations*. He was to be a fixture in the London musical world for many years, playing, teaching, composing, arranging, and editing. After his marriage, he received every important musician who came to London in his home, was entertained everywhere, and, despite so much work and so much social life, was a copious letter writer and kept a diary. He also liked, in free moments, to attend trials in the law courts and the debates in the Houses of Parliament. He once noted in his diary at the end of one year that he had in the past twelve months given 1457 lessons, 129 of them without charge. Other interesting events noted in the diary include its record of the appearance in 1821 of the metronome invented by J. N. Mälzel and visits to the piano factory of Sebastien Érard in Paris. Here he played on the instrument that incorporated many changes, but he did not adopt its use for some years, thus losing the distinction, which, a year or two later, fell to Liszt, of being the first to play it in public. He also at this time wrote in his diary an account of his performing Beethoven's *Choral Fantasy* and being accused of having composed the choruses himself.

In 1823, Moscheles returned to Vienna, where Beethoven lent him his Broadwood piano to use at a concert. It was then that he visited his old teacher, Salieri, in a hospital and received from the dying man the tearful request that he give the lie to the story, hardly credited but widely circulated as gossip, that Salieri had poisoned Mozart. The following year in Berlin, Moscheles met the Mendelssohn family and gave lessons to the fifteen-year-old Felix, who was to become his dearest friend. He also admired the playing, particularly in the music of Bach, of Felix's sister, Fanny Mendelssohn. He wrote in his diary that he taught Felix Mendelssohn "without losing sight for a single moment of the fact that I was sitting next to a master, not a pupil."

In Hamburg in 1825 Moscheles married Charlotte Embden, whom he described as a "fair" pianist. She returned with him to London where she shared his busy life. Moscheles jotted down themes for his compositions while walking from the house of one pupil to that of another. He went on Sundays to visit Clementi and his wife. While he called himself a pupil of Clementi, it is hard to believe that the old master had much to teach him at this stage of Moscheles' development.

Some of the pieces that Moscheles composed and performed at this time were highly popular products such as a fantasia on *Rule Brittania* and one on Irish themes. He gave tours in the provinces and composed, whenever he could find a spare moment, what he called his "fugitive" pieces, for which he received thirty guineas ($157) apiece. By 1827, he was earning two guineas ($10.50) an hour as a teacher, twice the fee that Clementi used to charge. Soon afterwards he wrote that Clementi, then about eighty, "extemporized with all the freshness of youth."

Moscheles first heard the teen-age prodigy, Franz Liszt, play in London the same year and wrote that he "surpasses in power and mastery of difficulties everything I have ever heard." Liszt's fantastic success never really was a threat to Moscheles, for England was the one country where it never really took hold. Liszt reappeared there only a few times, and, so far as the London public was concerned, Moscheles remained "the prince of pianists," as he was called, for many years.

The Moscheles diaries are full of fascinating accounts of happenings both sad and pleasant, such as his presence at the deathbed of Carl Maria von Weber in 1826 and, in the following year, his involvement with Beethoven during the master's last illness. At this time Moscheles persuaded the Philharmonic Society, of which he was now a member, to send the dying composer a hundred pounds ($500) in advance of a projected concert for his benefit. He entertained at home all the glamorous singers of the day, and became a kind of musical entrepreneur to the Rothschild family in London, arranging musical evenings with the great musicians of the time and receiving for his own services forty pounds every time he performed. His relations with the musician who was the most famous of all in those years, the violinist Nicolò Paganini, were friendly at first but ended in a threatened lawsuit over performance rights to transcriptions Moscheles had made of some Paganini violin pieces. Like everybody else, Moscheles was dazzled by Paganini's playing, but they were temperamental opposites and musicians of very different character. Moscheles wrote that Paganini's playing of the Beethoven *Kreutzer Sonata* was "a desecration."

In 1832, Moscheles conducted the Beethoven *Missa Solemnis* at a private performance, and five years later he conducted the Philharmonic Society in the Beethoven Ninth Symphony, a work that, though it had been commissioned by the Society, had never until then been popular in England. Moscheles was to conduct it again several times in later years and is credited with being the one who established it in the repertory.

After first encountering the music of Chopin, Moscheles declared that it was "not the work of a profound musician." Though he revised this opinion after meeting Chopin in Paris and hearing him play, he never truly liked this kind of piano music. His candidate as the greatest composer of his time was Mendelssohn, with whom he often performed in public and for whom his second son was named (the first died in infancy).

It was in 1832 that Moscheles finally adopted the use of the new and greatly improved Érard piano with its metal reinforcements and revolutionary action. Previously, he had been loyal to the Clementi piano, though he occasionally used those of Graf and Streicher.

The credit for giving the first recital made up entirely of piano music performed by one person usually goes to Liszt, who was the first to give such recitals regularly. However, Moscheles appears to have been the first to give such a recital in London, in 1837, though he did not make it a practice and generally kept to the custom of having well-known singers appear with him.

Although Moscheles constantly advocated the cause of the great masters and performed their works whenever possible, he had to go on supplying the public with new compositions that would serve for the "novelties" they demanded. He always deplored the public taste, which, during the first half of the nineteenth century, seemed to get worse instead of better. On returning to Vienna in 1844, he was horrified to discover that it was Donizetti and not Beethoven who was the rage there. He wrote in his diary: "The fashionable taste is a vitiated one, people will only listen to light music and easy rhythms."

Moscheles did play two-piano works with Liszt once or twice on the continent, and he appears never to have felt any jealousy of him. Once, when he received a visit from Liszt, he was astonished to discover that Liszt could read at sight the extremely difficult studies that he, Moscheles, had been composing. He was also deeply impressed by the playing of

Clara Wieck, later Clara Schumann, and once performed a Bach Three Piano Concerto with her and Mendelssohn. He heard the young prodigy, Anton Rubinstein, who was to become the greatest virtuoso after Liszt, and wrote about "his fingers as light as feathers, and with them the strength of a man."

To add to the prestige that he always maintained with the London public, Moscheles was made official pianist to Prince Albert, consort to Queen Victoria, who came to the throne in 1838. The Moscheles School of Piano Playing, which includes his many *études*, was dedicated to Prince Albert, thus giving the royal couple a brace of such works, since Karl Czerny dedicated his to the queen.

When he was in his mid-forties, Moscheles began to think about retirement from public performances. His diary for the years after 1840 takes note, quite objectively, of certain slights from princes and fellow musicians on the continent, where he spent two or three months every summer. He never actually admitted that his day was passing, but he seems to have been aware of it. Having been considered a dashing bravura player in his youth, it must have been bewildering for him to discover that, thanks mostly to improved pianos, younger virtuosos were even more dashing and could play with greater bravura. After one visit with Liszt, he recorded his conclusion that it was all due to the fact that the new generation had larger hands.

In 1846, Moscheles finally accepted Mendelssohn's repeated offer to become head of the department for playing and composition at the Leipzig Conservatory, which Mendelssohn had founded three years before. The eldest of Moscheles' three daughters had married, and he and his wife were attracted by the idea of returning to a Germanic country. Furthermore, he had become genuinely interested in musical education while serving as a part-time teacher at the London Royal Academy of Music, which had become important under the patronage of the musical Prince Consort.

Just a year after the Moscheles family settled in Leipzig,

on November 4, 1847, Mendelssohn died at the age of thirty-eight. Moscheles, who had kept watch at his deathbed, was a pallbearer at his funeral. Deeply grieved, he gave a great deal of his time and energy in the years that followed to editing and promoting Mendelssohn's works. Though he gave but few public performances, he continued to work on his playing and, in 1852, was inspired by the gift of a new and even more improved grand piano from the Érard firm. Thirteen years later, he reappeared in London and, in a concert at St. James Hall, excited his audience with a twenty-minute improvisation on *See the Conquering Hero Comes.*

Moscheles attended the premières of Wagner's *Lohengrin* and *Die Meistersinger* and was present during the Berlioz week that Liszt gave at Weimar; but the music of these two great composers bewildered him more than it impressed him. Jacques Barzun pointed out the irony of this in his definitive study of Berlioz when he wrote: "Berlioz' counterpoint seemed to Moscheles inexcusably free, whereas for us that of Moscheles is quite excusably dead."

One young composer to whom Moscheles gave his unqualified approval was Charles Gounod, who created the opera *Faust.* Since Moscheles considered himself a musical reformer and had been one in his youth, it was distressing for him to find himself in the reactionary position. So, he tried to keep abreast of change, but failed to do so. He was always a generous reactionary, however, and never was guilty, like Antonio Salieri and the famous composer and director of the Paris Conservatoire, Luigi Cherubini, of working to suppress the works of new and revolutionary composers.

During his last years, Moscheles was much honored and respected in Leipzig. His firm but kindly character made him ideally suited to his duties as teacher and administrator. His international prestige brought distinction to the new conservatory, in which his chief associate was the violinist, Ferdinand David, for whom Mendelssohn composed his violin concerto. Moscheles lived long enough to see the general improvement in musical taste that began to appear after the sobering anti-authoritarian uprisings that took place in France and Germany in 1848. His beloved Beethoven was at last widely recognized as a great master, the works of Bach had been rediscovered, and the public, faced with such serious "novelties" as the operas of Wagner and Verdi, was willing to fall back upon the masterpieces of the past instead of demanding the flashy bravura pieces that were all the fashion during the first half of the century.

Edward Dannreuther, who was a Moscheles pupil, wrote: "As a pianist, Moscheles was distinguished by a crisp and incisive touch, clear and precise phrasing, and pronounced preference for minute accentuation. He played octaves with stiff wrists and was chary in the use of the pedals."

It was appropriate that, in addition to his many other services to music, Moscheles should have been the one to translate into English the first important biography of Beethoven.

Franz Liszt
1811=1886

HALLEY'S comet was flashing its way across the sky on October 22, 1811, when Franz Liszt was born at Raiding, Hungary. Liszt was often compared to that comet, for his career was truly meteoric.

Adam Liszt, Franz's father, was a steward in the service of the Esterházy princes of Hungary. The Esterházys had a strong tradition of patronizing music and musicians, for their court had become known as one of the most musical in Europe when it was under the musical direction of "Poppa" Haydn, who died two years before Franz Liszt was born. Professional musicians in the employ of the Esterházy nobles not only performed and composed; they taught and played with the many members of the nobility who were amateur musicians. Adam Liszt, though not a noble but merely a steward, was known as a good amateur pianist. When it became evident, very early in life, that Adam's son had gifts far beyond the ordinary, nobody was surprised and everybody was interested. Adam gave Franz his first lessons and instructed him carefully at the piano and in the basics of theory and harmony. When Franz was only nine his father decided that he was ready to be presented to the world. Franz played at court to a group of the most powerful nobles of Hungary, all of whom were musicians or music lovers. So startling was the boy's effect on these men that they decided he must be given the finest possible training; and they immediately got up a fund that guaranteed the security of the Liszt family for some years to come. Adam took his wife and son to Vienna, where Franz was put in the charge of Karl Czerny, who recognized that in young Liszt he had found the perfect subject for his teaching. The boy was a diligent and devoted pupil, and his progress was all that Czerny could hope for. Franz also was instructed in composition by the Italian composer, Antonio Salieri, who was soon to become the first director of the Vienna Conservatory.

When Liszt was still only eleven, Czerny decided that he was ready to play in public. His first appearance created the excitement that only the playing of a fabulously gifted prodigy can do. At his second appearance, some days later, a great many important people came to hear him, including Beethoven, who was deaf and aging but curious about his friend Czerny's discovery; and skeptical, too, probably, for he had seen many prodigies come and go. However, after the concert, Beethoven, the great man of music, went up to the boy and embraced him. Liszt never forgot this. Beethoven became and remained his god, one that he was to serve well in later years, after Beethoven died and his music still was not accepted, as it is today, as perhaps the greatest ever composed.

Liszt's career as a composer began at this time in an interesting way. The publishing firm of Coppi & Diabelli, headed by Antonio Diabelli, an amateur musician, decided to publish a set of variations on a theme by Diabelli that would be composed by all the important composers in Vienna at the time. Liszt, by far the youngest of the lot, was asked to do the twenty-second variation. There were fifty-one variations in all, each by a different composer. Eventually, the whole set was published together with Beethoven's opus 120, his thirty-three variations on the same theme of Diabelli, one of his last great works for the piano. Thus, Liszt, at the beginning of his career, was linked with Beethoven, who was nearing the end of his.

Since Paris was in those days the music center of Europe, Adam Liszt decided, upon the advice of others, that Franz should go there to study at the famous conservatory, then considered the finest in existence. Prince Metternich, that most powerful and crafty of politicians, had taken an interest in the talented young Liszt and gave his father a letter of commendation that should have served to open every door in Paris to Adam and his son. However, Metternich had underestimated the intransigence of Luigi Cherubini, the tyrannical director of the Paris Conservatoire. Though he was himself foreign born, Cherubini refused to waive the rule against admission of foreigners to the conservatory of Paris. Poor Cherubini, who was a very distinguished composer of the old school, for years was remembered less for that than as the man who resisted all change and opposed some of the most important musical innovators of the century.

Though his mission in Paris had failed, Adam Liszt decided to remain there and have Franz taught privately. Paris became home to young Liszt, and his formative years were spent there. He was to meet and know all the important musicians of the time and, in addition, many famous writers such as Lamartine and Victor Hugo, from whom he acquired the literary inclinations that permeated his works. Most of his compositions were to have a literary impetus and were given literary subjects. Critics have claimed that in Liszt this was affectation, part of his pandering to the taste of the times. But to an unprejudiced observer, it appears to have been a genuine part of Liszt's personality; and it seems that he was truly dependent on a literary stimulus to produce musical ideas. Thus, his finest piano work, the lengthy *Années de Pèlerinage*, is divided into many separate pieces bearing such titles as *Three Sonnets of Petrarch* and *After a Lecture of Dante*.

Liszt was still only twelve, though already something of a musical celebrity in Paris, when he adopted the use of the new pianoforte developed by Sebastien Érard, whose new Grand Piano Forte, as it was called in public announcements, had been patented in 1821. Érard's first pianoforte, built in

1770, was a square with five octaves. His original grand piano was built in 1796 and was the first of its kind to be used in France. The new piano that Liszt introduced at concerts in London and Paris had seven octaves and incorporated an important new development, the double escarpment or "repetition" action, which increased the speed at which a hammer could be used, released, and used again, and which greatly improved the player's control of both staccato and legato effects.

Despite his growing fame as a pianist, young Liszt was more interested in his future as a composer and did not at the time envision for himself a career as a great virtuoso. He was busy composing an operetta, *Don Sancho,* which was produced in Paris at the Académie Royale in October, 1825, one week before his fourteenth birthday. This work was not particularly successful, though it added to his reputation. The manuscript later was destroyed in a fire, so we are unable to judge its merits today. Liszt might have gone on thinking of himself mainly as a composer and bent all his efforts in that direction were it not for the fact that his father died before he was sixteen, leaving the boy to support himself and his mother. Adam Liszt had been careful not to exploit Franz as a performer and had restricted his public performances. Now, however, there was nothing for Franz to do but take up the life of a performing artist, which promised to pay well, while that of a composer hardly paid at all. Still, being a perfectionist, he thought himself unready to meet all the challenges of competition with established virtuosos; and the new Érard piano presented problems that it would take time for him to solve. So, he began to take pupils and to play at concerts whenever he got the chance. These were restless, uncertain years in his life, which marked the difficult transition from youth to manhood.

One of the most important events of Liszt's life took place when he was nineteen, at the Paris Opéra where he heard a concert given by the dazzling Italian violinist, Nicolò Paganini. This concert, and his subsequent friendship with Paganini, changed his life. Many critics have thought that it changed his life for the worse, though it generally is acknowledged that it was through Paganini's influence and example that Liszt set himself the goal of becoming the greatest pianist of his time.

Nicolò Paganini was twenty-seven years older than Liszt. He had become a legend in his own lifetime and, in the end, was the victim of that legend, since many people accepted as fact that part of it that claimed he had made a pact with the devil. Perhaps the same could be said of Liszt, though if he was the victim of his own legend, it was in a different way; and he, recognizing the danger, made a great effort to avoid it. One writer on Liszt called him "a greathearted charlatan," which is fair enough in a way but does not tell us the whole story. Liszt lived in a time that was heavily and showily romantic, the post-Napoleonic era, in which the old aristocracy was losing its power and yielding its prerogatives to the rising middle class. As a result, the aristocrats had become less realistic, more arrogant, and essentially escapist. Their values had become exaggerated, and they took delight in theatrical effects, whether or not there was anything substantial behind them. This was the public that Liszt set out to please and capture. No doubt, Paganini knew all about this and explained it to Liszt, advising him to do as he had done, which was to cultivate flamboyance and show in order to engage and hold the attention of the aristocracy. The middle class, still unsure of itself, imitated the aristocracy in all things and would follow their lead. So, Liszt set about the business of cultivating lords and ladies, which gave him the name of a snob. Perhaps this was justified, though it seems more likely that he had accepted the necessity to be an opportunist since that was the easiest if not the only way to promote himself and his talents. Though he learned his lessons from Paganini well, he was in fact very different from him in personality. Paganini was a macabre, emaciated man who suffered from continual illnesses and had a dark, brooding side to his nature, which lent some credibility to the rumors about his supposed diabolism. These rumors were, of course, nonsense; but Paganini considered them good publicity and so played upon them to his own advantage, though after his death, they resulted in his being denied Christian burial. Liszt, on the other hand, was a cheerful, healthy, outgoing person with boundless energy and enthusiasm. Though he did in fact become the Paganini of the piano, his life was a happier and fuller one than that of the great violinist. There is nothing strange about a youth of nineteen being so much influenced by an older man who was the idol of the era. Perhaps Liszt accepted Paganini's advice cynically or perhaps he turned to him at a time when he greatly needed someone to replace the father he had lost.

For the next two years, Liszt played in public but seldom and gave himself up to a period of intense study. During this time, he earned money by giving lessons. At the end of this period, he emerged as a virtuoso of a kind never before encountered among pianists. The public, realizing this, discovered him all over again. He had rivals, of course, of which the most formidable was the German pianist, Sigismund Thalberg.

Thalberg, a pupil of J. N. Hummel and Ignaz Moscheles, was the illegitimate son of a count and a baroness. He had been a schoolmate of Napoleon's son, the unhappy Duke of Reichstadt who was called "L'Aiglon" and had been proclaimed King of Rome by his father. Thalberg, ever conscious of his aristocratic heritage and high-level connections, cultivated poise, calm, and reserve for his platform manner. He supposedly rehearsed his stage bow for years, until he had got into it just the right combination of aloofness, superiority, and gracious acknowledgment of the audience's adulation. Part of his appeal to the public came from the knowledge that he was, above all else, a "gentleman."

The Paris music journals began to print articles about the comparative merits of Liszt and Thalberg, and the rivalry between them soon became a public preoccupation. In 1837, when it was at its height, the two pianists were persuaded to engage in a musical duel. They played in competition in several salons of the Paris ruling class, usually for the benefit of some worthy charity. The climactic engagement took place in the salon of an eccentric Italian princess. She was a passionate partisan of Italian independence and was involved in secret plots to free her native city of Milan from the Austrians. She also was known for her behavior at concerts, to which she came dressed as a nun but with lilies in her hair, and during which she usually swooned.

The aristocracy paid eight dollars apiece to attend the competition in the princess' salon. Thalberg played a fantasy on themes from Rossini's *Moisè* and Liszt one on Paër's *Niobe*. Liszt was proclaimed the winner, which meant that he became the pet of the music patrons who made and unmade reputations. Thalberg, of course, was annoyed at having to take second place, but his popularity throughout Europe continued. In 1856, he gave a tour in the United States, thus becoming one of the first famous virtuosos to do so. Thalberg, despite his defeat in the competition with Liszt, appeared with him in a concert a few days later when he was one of six pianists who performed together in variations on themes from Bellini's *I Puritani*. Among the other players were Frédéric Chopin and Karl Czerny. This sort of performance was typical of the times. The vogue for the piano as an instrument for display rather than serious musical interpretation was at its height. Almost everybody who had the price was taking piano lessons, and several inventions to facilitate technical dexterity were in fashion. This also was the period during which there were short-lived vogues for pianos with stops that produced bassoon, harp, or mandoline effects and had drums, bells, and cymbals attached. At this time, too, the rage for waltzes had begun and was to be followed by that for polkas.

Though Liszt was a master of the classic repertory, that is, of Mozart, Beethoven, and, eventually, Chopin, his programs from this time forth featured the transcriptions, mostly of opera arias, that his public adored. They always clamored for more, and Liszt gave them more. The number of transcriptions he made of everything from Bellini to Wagner is astonishing. They feature every known trick of the virtuoso's trade and many new ones that Liszt invented. Some of these transcriptions seem ridiculous to us today, but others, if listened to without prejudice, are exciting and of considerable musical interest.

Whatever Liszt stood for in public, his personal taste and discernment were of the finest; and though he may have sacrificed his ideals for the sake of popular success, he preserved them in other ways, particularly when it came to recognizing and supporting other composers. One of his most important friendships was with the great French composer, Hector Berlioz, whom he met in 1830 after a concert at which Berlioz' *Symphonie fantastique* was performed. This friendship lasted until Berlioz' death in 1869. Berlioz, whose music was scorned by all but a few, made a precarious living as a musical journalist. He was a severe critic, but his praise of Liszt was unstinting and helped to make him famous. Liszt, in return, was one of Berlioz' most generous and effective supporters. In 1834, Berlioz took Liszt to the salon of the Countess d'Agoult. This was a fateful meeting, for Liszt and the Countess fell in love and made a life together for the next twelve years. Though legal and religious difficulties made it impossible for them to marry, they had three children, a son and two daughters, only one of which, his daughter Cosima, survived Liszt.

Another of Liszt's important friendships began in 1831, when he and Frédéric Chopin met for the first time. This was a somewhat uneasy relationship, for Chopin, who was ill and beset by problems, sometimes resented Liszt's great popularity and money-making abilities. However, Chopin could not resist Liszt's good-heartedness and powers as a pianist. He once said that he had never really heard some of his own compositions until he heard Liszt play them. The two men once played together at a joint recital, which was a mistake, for Chopin, whose physical weakness handicapped him, was a pianist only for the salon. His fortes were said to have been the equivalent of Liszt's pianissimos, and at their concert, his playing was almost inaudible, while Liszt, as usual, stormed the rafters and got all the applause. But Chopin, of course, was a great and unique composer, a fact that Liszt recognized with the generosity and lack of envy that he always showed toward composers of genius. It is surprising to realize that Liszt knew and acknowledged the importance of so many composers who now are considered among the greatest in history. Rossini, Beethoven, Schubert, Mendelssohn, Schumann, Brahms, Berlioz, Chopin, Verdi, Wagner: Liszt knew them all, was affected by all of them, and had some effect on each of them.

It was Liszt who, at the Countess d'Agoult's salon, introduced Chopin to the famous woman novelist who called herself George Sand, thereby precipitating another famous romance. The Countess d'Agoult imitated Mme. Sand by adopting a man's name, Daniel Stern, by writing novels herself, which were inferior to those of her friend, and by cultivating a reputation for eccentricity.

From 1839 to 1847, Liszt lived the life of a great virtuoso, touring almost constantly, receiving the nearly hysterical adulation of the public, and being received in all the great salons of Europe. There is no doubt that he had a magnetic appeal to the public. His portraits that are most familiar to us today are those of an old man with warts; but in his youth, he was romantically handsome. He learned to add to his romantic atmosphere by using dramatic facial expressions and growing his hair to a length that would enable him to toss it about effectively at appropriate moments. He also sported a chest full of medals and decorations that clanked as he marched to the piano but undoubtedly added to the effect. The public demanded more and more of him—greater and more overpowering virtuoso effects—so that, in the end, he must have felt like the matador from whom the public demands more and more until, at last, he is fatally gored by the bull. At any rate, Liszt, who performed regularly in Paris, Berlin, Leipzig, Copenhagen, Constantinople, Madrid, Lisbon, Budapest, Warsaw, Moscow, and St. Petersburg, as well as in countless lesser cities, gave up his virtuoso's career at the age of thirty-six. The only city of Europe in which he was coldly received was London, where he had been successful as a child. This was because of public disapproval of his irregular relationship with the Countess. When a London impresario lost money on him, Liszt, in a characteristic gesture, paid the losses from his own pocket.

Though he undoubtedly pandered to the public taste, Liszt did persuade his admirers to listen to music to which they had been indifferent by playing transcriptions of such works as the fifth, sixth, and seventh symphonies of Beethoven and the *Symphonie fantastique* of Berlioz. And, despite his reputation for never playing good music in public, he did give, at various times, performances of such monumental piano works as the Bach *Goldberg Variations*, the last Beethoven sonatas and concertos, the Schubert *Wanderer Fantasy*, Schumann's *Carnaval*, the Mendelssohn concertos, and almost everything composed by Chopin.

Liszt had several good reasons for abandoning his career as a pianist. He had earned a fortune; no doubt he was weary of public life and appalled by his own legend; he longed to compose more and greater works; and he had begun a new career as *Kapellmeister* to the Grand Duke of Weimar. Perhaps the most persuasive reason came from the fact that his relationship with the Countess had failed and he had, in 1847, formed a new relationship with the Polish Princess Karolyn Sayn-Wittgenstein, who probably encouraged him to make this radical change in his life, not only for his sake, but for her own as well. Liszt played his last public concert in the Russian city of Elisavetgrad that December. He never again played for a fee, though he did play in public again occasionally, usually without being announced and on the spur of the moment.

Stories about Liszt as a performer and public personality are legion. It was said when he retired that he did so because the public was turning against him. This may have been true to some extent, since tastes were changing and he had been before the public long enough to wear out his welcome as a "novelty." He was supposed to have been a great destroyer of pianos. No doubt his instruments, which, though reinforced by metal, were hardly equal to the modern Steinway, gave out from time to time. He is supposed to have said once, in a paraphrase of Louis XIV's famous claim about the state, *le concert, c'est moi,* which, on the face of it, was true at the time. However, it seems likely that this was a bit of weary irony on Liszt's part rather than a mark of fatuous egotism. In 1842, he gave a series of twenty-one recitals in rapid succession in Berlin and, when he left town in a carriage drawn by six horses, was followed like a king by a great procession. A year later he found that the Berlin public had cooled toward him, and it probably was then that he began to think seriously about retiring. It must have been hard for a man to keep his equilibrium after, as had happened in Budapest, being presented with a patent of nobility and a jeweled sword after his concert and then being escorted home by twenty thousand people carrying lighted torches.

Liszt usually played extemporaneously on themes suggested by his audiences and carried with him a silver chalice, supposedly made by Cellini, which he placed in the concert-hall lobbies for the purpose of collecting the slips on which members of the audience suggested themes. Though he was accustomed to performing for audiences of five or six hundred people and in St. Petersburg appeared before fifteen hundred, he once, in Leipzig, found himself unexpectedly confronted by a very small audience. After surveying the situation, he invited the small group to adjourn to his hotel, where he played to them in the greater comfort and intimacy of his suite. Another delightful Liszt story concerns a young woman, who, though she had never met him, advertised herself as a Liszt pupil, little knowing that he was in the town where she was to play her debut concert. Just before it was to begin, she was astonished to receive a visit from him. He asked her to play for him, offered a few suggestions, and then told her that she could now in all honesty claim him as her teacher.

Two examples will suffice to illustrate the limitations that the public imposed on Liszt. Once, at a Milan concert, while he was performing one of his études, a man in the audience called out: "I came here to be entertained, not to hear somebody practice." Another time, in Paris at the Salle de Conservatoire, he was playing the Beethoven *Kreutzer Sonata* with the distinguished violinist, Lambert Massart. In the middle of a movement, somebody demanded that Liszt play his Fantasy on Meyerbeer's *Robert le Diable*. The audience took up the cry, increasing its clamor as Liszt resisted, until he was forced to comply while poor Massart stood helplessly by.

When Liszt retired as a pianist, he left behind him many changes in piano technique for which he was directly responsible. He was the first and one of the most sensational of modern piano virtuosos. Any piano student confronted by one of his *Transcendental Études* can see for himself what sort of pianist Liszt was. It has been said that he was the first pianist who could produce a gigantic tone without sacrificing the quality of that tone. Many of his pupils, attempting to emulate him, produced the quantity without the quality and led subsequent generations to believe, wrongly, that Liszt was a piano pounder. Liszt supposedly changed notes to suit his own convenience and to create difficulties where none existed for the sake of show. Perhaps the public demanded this of him, which may have been one reason why he played Beethoven and Chopin less and less through the years and concentrated on his own compositions and transcriptions.

One of Liszt's innovations was his use of a higher piano stool. He played from the shoulders rather than the wrists. He also was one of the first to turn the piano sideways. Though Liszt, like Dussek before him, was accused of doing this to display his profile, it seems more likely that he had discovered the music sounded better that way. Liszt also was the first pianist regularly to give solo recitals, that is, without orchestral, vocal, or chamber interludes to give variety to the programs.

One of Liszt's activities during the period of his greatest fame was on behalf of the Beethoven Memorial at Bonn. He raised most of the money for the statue at benefit concerts and was the organizer of the dedication concerts at Bonn in 1845. Liszt realized that the memorial, which, until he took over, could not be financed, was important because it would attract attention to Beethoven's music, which still was resisted by a large portion of the public, particularly in France. One can imagine that Liszt, who knew the value of publicity, believed that as soon as a composer had been immortalized in stone, his music would cease to be controversial and become immortal, too.

After 1847, Liszt lived mainly at Weimar. With the duke's patronage, he established a music center there that was, while it lasted, one of the most important in Europe. He was able to compose, produce new operatic and symphonic works by other composers, some of which he conducted himself, and to teach. Piano pupils came from everywhere; and he taught them all for free. He seemed to be unable to say no to any reasonably talented pianist who presented himself at Weimar. Eventually, the magic formula—"pupil of Liszt"—was advertised by piano teachers in the major cities of Europe and America.

Surrounded as he was by pupils, admirers, court officials, visiting composers, society ladies, and sychophants, it is hard to understand how Liszt managed to compose. But he did, and in enormous quantities. Unfortunately, his best known compositions, such as *Liebestraum* and the *Hungarian Rhapsody#2,* are his most superficial. His most ambitious works, skillful and dramatic as they are, have faded from the repertory, though his *Faust* and *Dante* symphonies have been revived with some success of late, and there are conductors who are very partial to them. His songs, long forgotten, recently have been rediscovered and turn out to be lovely and distinguished. One reason for their neglect is that their accompaniments, composed as they were by a fabulous virtuoso, are so difficult to play.

The most famous of Liszt's many associations with great composers is the one with Richard Wagner, which began in 1840 in Paris when Wagner was a struggling and obscure young composer who had gone there to seek his fortune. However, Paris was not for him, and he soon departed. He and Liszt did not meet again for some years, though they corresponded. In 1848, when Wagner was forced to flee from Dresden, where he was *Kapellmeister,* because of his revolutionary activities, he took refuge with Liszt at Weimar. But this was still Germany, and not even Liszt could get Wagner excused for political offenses. So, Wagner was forced to flee again, this time to Switzerland. Liszt did the best thing he could do for him, which was to produce his operas at Weimar. He gave *The Flying Dutchman* and *Tannhäuser* and, on August 20, 1850, the world première of *Lohengrin,* which he conducted himself.

Two years later, Liszt gave a Berlioz week at Weimar, during which he produced Berlioz' neglected opera, *Benvenuto Cellini.* He also secured from the Grand Duke a commission for Wagner to compose his *Siegfried's Tod,* which eventually became the four operas of the *Ring* cycle that were produced not under the auspices of the Grand Duke of Weimar but of the King of Bavaria. Many other new or neglected works were sponsored by Liszt during his years at Weimar. When, in 1859, he finally gave up his post, it was because of opposition to his production of a new work, Peter Cornelius' *The Barber of Bagdad.*

During the last twenty-five years of his life, Liszt divided his time between Weimar, Rome, and Budapest. In Budapest he became director of a musical institute founded by the Hungarian government in his honor. In 1879, he took religious orders in Rome, becoming Abbé Liszt. Much has been written about his motive for joining the tertiary order of St. Francis, but one assumes that, whatever his motive was, it was perfectly sincere. However, it has been suggested that he took the step in order to avoid marrying Princess Sayn-Wittgenstein, who for years had been petitioning Rome for an annulment of her marriage and now had some hope of getting one. More likely, Liszt, who as a child had been dissuaded from becoming a priest, found spiritual satisfaction when he joined the order, though it can not be said that after this event his life was changed very much.

If in later years Liszt found himself in the shadow of Wagner, he showed no signs of resenting it. Instead, he was delighted by Wagner's hard-won success and had nothing but the most intense admiration for his operas. However, when Liszt's daughter, Cosima, renounced her religion so as to obtain a divorce from her husband, Hans von Bülow, and marry Wagner, Liszt was shocked. He and the Wagners were estranged for three years. The reconciliation came about in 1873 when Wagner was conducting a campaign for funds to build a *festspielhaus* in which his operas would be performed. Liszt, with his unfailing generosity, responded to the crusade by joining it and helping to raise the money. He attended the opening performance of the Bayreuth Festspielhaus in 1876 and was part of an audience that included many members of the nobility, the philosopher Nietzsche, and the composer Tchaikovsky. In his last opera, *Parsifal,* produced at Bayreuth in 1882, Wagner paid his father-in-law the compliment of borrowing note for note the opening theme of his B-Minor Sonata as the theme for Kundry, the opera's heroine.

Not that Liszt went unhonored himself. Budapest held festivals in his honor, during which his religious choral works were performed; and, in the last year of his life, London also gave a festival of his works. In this city where, years before, he had had his only real experience of failure, he was cheered in the streets and acclaimed everywhere he went. During one concert of his works, he was persuaded to play, and it was said that at seventy-five his playing was more beautiful than ever.

Liszt, who was but two years older than Wagner, was greatly affected by Wagner's death, which occurred in Venice in 1883, just a few weeks after Liszt had visited him there. He outlived Wagner by three years. Perhaps it was significant and not ironic that Liszt's own death took place at Bayreuth a few hours after he had heard a performance of *Tristan und Isolde*. The last word that he ever spoke was "Tristan." Though many people thought that he should be buried in Budapest, Weimar, Paris, or Rome, Cosima insisted that it should be at Bayreuth, where Wagner was buried.

Cosima, Frau Wagner, became the guiding spirit of the Bayreuth festivals. She survived her father by forty-four years and was ninety-three when she died. Her son, Siegfried Wagner, was a disappointment; but her grandsons, Wieland and Wolfgang Wagner, completely revitalized Bayreuth after World War II. They brought new dimensions to the art of stage direction; and surely it can be supposed that these two grandsons of Richard Wagner, who were so gifted dramatically, derived some share of their theatrical instincts from their great-grandfather, who was Franz Liszt.

~II~

Clara Schumann

1819=1896

———◆———

THOUGH not the first great woman pianist, nor the only one of her time, Clara Wieck Schumann was certainly the most famous, for she had a long and distinguished career and was closely associated with two of the greatest composers of the nineteenth century, one of whom was her husband.

She was a reformer, partly by nature and partly through circumstances. The woman who said of Franz Liszt that "he has the decline of pianoforte playing on his conscience" was destined to become one of those pianists who chose to be "interpreters" rather than "performers" and, in so doing, created a new standard for their art. It never can be truly established whether circumstances create the man (or woman) or vice versa, so it can not be said whether Clara Schumann and others like her forced the public to accept their standards or merely came along when the public was ready for them. Certainly, by the time Clara was a mature artist, there was a vacuum that she was able to fill. Most of the music that now constitutes the standard piano repertory already had been composed; but, so far as the general public was concerned, it was neglected and unknown. When the tide turned in the middle of the nineteenth century and serious music finally took preference over ephemeral transcriptions, potpourris, and fantasias based on operatic arias and

Viennese waltzes, it was Clara Schumann who got a good deal of the credit for "educating" the public taste. She was indeed a *grande dame* of music, the implacable enemy of all that she considered false, tawdry, or merely superficial, who earned her high reputation by performing the music of Bach, Beethoven, Chopin, and, particularly, Schumann and Brahms. It was not that she swept everything before her and rose triumphant above the wreckage of all that was superficial. The war went on to the end of her life, and she was forever engaged in resisting and deploring the popularity of Liszt and his school, the success of later virtuosos like Anton Rubinstein, and, especially, the enormous influence of the operas of Richard Wagner.

In Leipzig, where Clara was born on September 13, 1819, her father, Friedrich Wieck, was a musician of importance. A noted teacher both of the piano and singing, he was a follower of the Logier system, established by Johann Bernhard Logier which became both popular and controversial in the early nineteenth century. This sytem involved the use of a simple machine called the chiroplast, which forced the hands into position at the keyboard. Logier also developed elaborate charts for teaching sight reading, and advocated the training of beginning piano pupils in groups rather than individually. Alwin Wieck, Clara's brother, and Marie Wieck, her sister, both became well-known pianists and important teachers in Dresden. Friedrich Wieck's most famous pupil, apart from Clara Schumann, was Hans von Bülow, a noted virtuoso and conductor, who was the first husband of Liszt's daughter, Cosima, and in 1875 became one of the first modern virtuosos to tour in America.

Clara Wieck made her first public appearance at the age of seven and gave her first tour in Germany at thirteen. However, it was in Vienna in 1837, when she was not yet eighteen, that her fame was really established. At this debut, which took place ten years after the death of Beethoven, she played several of his sonatas, including the now famous *Apassionata*. The Viennese public had almost forgotten its

great composer; and Clara Wieck, a scholarly but temperamental player and most attractive young woman, reminded
them to great effect. So strong an impression did she make,
that the leading poet of Vienna, Franz Grillparzer, immortalized her in verse.

Clara Wieck was only eleven when her father received as
a pupil at Leipzig the young Robert Schumann, the son of a
bookseller, who had finally given up the study of law to seek
a career in music. His ambition to be a pianist was thwarted
once and for all when one of his fingers was paralyzed as a
result, it was said, of a too rigid use of Logier's chiroplast.
Friedrich Wieck, knowing that Schumann could not hope
for a career as a pianist, did not think well of his prospects
as a composer, which may have been why he so bitterly opposed his daughter's marriage to him. The engagement of
Clara Wieck to Robert Schumann took place on August 14,
1837, a month before her eighteenth birthday and the day
after she had introduced at a Leipzig concert Schumann's
Études symphonique, op.13. The marriage was delayed for
three years because of Wieck's opposition but finally took
place on September 12, 1840. Schumann had finally overcome Wieck's opposition by taking him to court to show
cause why he should continue his objections. The judge decided in Schumann's favor.

Until 1856, Clara Schumann's life was devoted to her husband and his art. Though she had eight children, one of
which died in infancy, she found time to play in public occasionally, primarily to introduce new piano works of Schumann. They lived mostly in Leipzig, though later in Dresden.
Schumann, in addition to his activities as a composer, edited
an influential music magazine, for which he wrote articles
signed by such names as Florestan and Eusebius. These
were characters he used in his great piano work, *Carnaval,*
in which, as in his less familiar but equally wonderful *Da-
vidsbündlertänze,* he immortalized Clara as Chiarina. In his
articles and those by others in the magazine, Schumann
called for recognition of composers such as Berlioz, Chopin,

and, in later years, his young friend Johannes Brahms. The *Davidsbündler*, an imaginary group that he used in his critical writings as well as in his piano pieces, were in Schumann's mind an ardent band who opposed the forces of Philistinism. In 1844, Schumann's career as editor of the music magazine came to an end. In the same year he and Clara went on a concert tour in Russia. In 1850, the Schumanns moved to Düsseldorf from Dresden so that Robert could become city music director in collaboration with the pianist and conductor, Ferdinand Hiller. Schumann, who was naturally deeply sensitive, reserved, and even retiring, had always been subject to melancholia; by 1853, his symptoms became much worse, and he was forced to give up his post. The following year, he attempted suicide by leaping into the Rhine, but was rescued. The rest of his life was spent in an asylum at Endenich near Bonn. The doctors forbade Clara to see him, fearing that it would excite him too much, so she was dependent on friends, one of which was Brahms, for contact with him. She was forced to assume the burden of his support in the asylum as well as that of her seven children and so resumed her concert career.

Clara had first met Johannes Brahms in 1853, when she was thirty-four and he twenty-one. Her first public performance of a Brahms work was in Leipzig on October 23, 1854, when she played the andante and scherzo from his F-minor Sonata. The next year, she performed in the same concert with him in Danzig. Also appearing with them was the great violinist Joseph Joachim, who was to be the close associate of Clara and Brahms and their partner in the crusade for the best in music.

When Robert Schumann and his wife first received a call from Johannes Brahms in 1853, the enmity between the followers of Liszt and those who thought of themselves as classicists was already well established. Brahms' call symbolized his wish to join Schumann's camp, for he had just been at Weimar as Liszt's guest and had found the atmosphere, both musical and social, not to his liking. The story goes that

Brahms had wanted to depart from the Weimar circle but had not known how to make the break, a problem which was solved for him one evening when Liszt was playing his B-Minor Sonata to a gathering of his adherents and observed that Brahms was sound asleep. Deeply offended, Liszt stopped abruptly and left the room. Brahms left Weimar soon afterwards. However, Liszt was one who could not hold a grudge for long. He recognized Brahms' genius and later tried to bring him back into his circle. Brahms' animosity toward the Liszt school had nothing personal in it. He simply did not admire their theories and disliked the kind of formal society, with its affected manners, artistic snobbery, and flattering of the aristocracy, that prevailed at Weimar.

Robert Schumann, whose major piano works had been performed by Liszt, had much in common with Brahms, for he, too, had no wish to make his way in high society. He appears to have recognized Brahms' potential at once, for after their first meeting, he announced to Clara that "this is he that should come." He presumably meant that Brahms was to be the next in the great line of composers from Bach through Beethoven and Schubert to Schumann himself. In this prediction he was correct, though he did not live to see it fulfilled. The lifelong friendship of Clara Schumann and Brahms is documented in their published correspondence, which, however, is far from complete, the more revealing letters having been destroyed by both parties. Thus, scholars and historians have never been able to determine whether the friendship was at any time a romance. Brahms was thirteen years younger than Clara. It seems obvious from their letters that he was in love with her at first but that, after Schumann's death when he might have married her, any question of romance had been settled, and not in his favor. Brahms remained her faithful friend for the rest of her life, visited her frequently, and gave much time and effort in her behalf. In 1856, he presented to Clara a sum of money gathered by her Leipzig friends and colleagues. Brahms wrote to Clara that this sum of money was "not a gift that they wish

to make you but an offering of love and gratitude to a respected artist." In April of the same year, Clara went on her
first tour in England, remaining for three months. She was
to make nineteen such tours in all. Though she received an
offer to go to America in 1861, she decided against it, and so
never went there. Following this first English tour, she met
Brahms at Antwerp and took him to Ostend so that he could
have his first look at the sea. After Schumann's death in
1856, Brahms remained with her at Düsseldorf for three
months. The following year, she moved to Berlin, where she
would have greater opportunities for teaching. Brahms, who
had lived mainly in Hamburg until then, settled in Vienna
soon afterwards. Clara was not happy in Berlin and in
1860, after giving a concert there, wrote to Brahms: "I can
only play the things I like to people who are sympathetic, so I
shall not play here again in a hurry."

The pianist Ignaz Moscheles described Clara's playing as
"void of all affectation." This did not mean that it was dull or
pedantic. She must have had plenty of romantic sweep to her
playing, even though she considered herself a classicist. Earlier, a woman of the aristocracy had written in a letter that
Clara "had the audacity to perform the whole of her program
by heart." She appears to have been one of the first to do so,
and her programs were long and unrelentingly serious. She
first performed the difficult and stormy First Piano Concerto
of Brahms with the Hamburg Philharmonic on December 3,
1861. It had not been a success when Brahms played it himself but became more popular through her performance. The
beautiful Second Concerto was not composed until 1882,
when Clara's public performances had become few and she
was past her prime as a virtuoso. So she was not the first
woman to play it in public. However, Clara pioneered for
Brahms by performing many of his piano works over and
over again and by participating in many performances of his
chamber works with other notable artists.

Once, after performing two Mozart concertos, Clara wrote
to Brahms: "You cannot imagine how sad I am when I feel I
have not put my heart into my playing. To me it is as if I had

done an injury not only to myself but also to art." To which Brahms replied: "The very public which is always pointing to Mozart and making fun of modern tawdriness, really only enjoys the latter and gets no pleasure whatever from the former." Later, after enjoying a triumph in Paris performing the Beethoven *Emperor* Concerto, she wrote to Brahms that she preferred Paris to London for the one reason that there the critics called on her, while in London she was expected to call on them. It was during this Paris visit that she acquired her favorite piano, a new and improved Érard. She was at her peak at this time and toured constantly, giving five concerts in four towns during one week. As a result of all this activity, so necessary for the support of her family, she was able to purchase a small house in Baden Baden, where she spent the summers for many years.

It was during this period, when Clara was at the height of her fame, that the enmity between her school of musical thought and that of the followers of Liszt reached its zenith. Brahms was the natural enemy of Richard Wagner, Liszt's protégé. Actually, Brahms did not seek this role or care for it very much; but it was thrust upon him by his friend and champion, the powerful Viennese critic Eduard Hanslick, who despised Wagner's operas. Wagner had his revenge on Hanslick when he obviously characterized him as Beckmesser in his *Die Meistersinger* (1868). Brahms, the violinist Joachim, and Clara were signers of an anti-Wagner, anti-Liszt manifesto in 1860. This was followed by a bitter split between the two camps with much discussion in the newspapers and musical journals. Wagner, to his eternal discredit, injected a nasty note of anti-Semitism into the controversy in an article that he published under a pseudonym. To us today it seems difficult to understand why one had to choose between Wagner's music and Brahms' and not be free to enjoy both, but such is the nature of art, or at least of its followers. Today we feel totally free to enjoy and admire the music of both masters and even to take pleasure in the more superficial music of the Liszt variety that was so much despised by Clara and Brahms. After hearing Wagner's *Tristan und Isolde* in Munich in 1875, ten years after its première, Clara wrote to Brahms: "That they should dare to offer such a piece to a cultured public, or to a public desiring to be cultured, is a terribly sad proof of the demoralization of the age. But even to think about it makes me boil with indignation." Even so, she later went to hear *Das Rheingold* and *Die Walküre*, going back a second time to the latter on the excuse that she wanted to "study the instrumentation."

One of Clara's interesting appearances was when she performed Schumann's Andante and Variations, op.46 for two pianos with her daughter Elise at her debut. She later performed the same work in Vienna with Brahms. She played almost every year in London, both with the Philharmonic Society, most often in the Schumann Concerto, and at the Popular Concerts. She gave a Russian tour in 1864. One of her most popular performances was of the Chopin F Minor Concerto. She and Joachim often played the Brahms violin sonatas and she also played in his piano quartets and quintets with Joachim's quartet, most frequently in London.

In 1872, the year in which tragedy began to close in upon her again, Clara's constant need to provide for her large family was somewhat alleviated by a fund established by friends that provided a substantial capital. Her daughter, Julie, died in this year and her son, Ludwig, had to be sent to an asylum. These tragedies were followed by others. Her youngest son, Felix, died in 1879 and her third son, Ferdinand, in 1891. Ferdinand's long illness and incapacity made it necessary for Clara to take care of his wife and several children. Another tragedy that affected her deeply was the death of a grandchild. Furthermore, rheumatic pains in her shoulders and hands and trouble with her hearing made it difficult for Clara to play. But she never gave up and reappeared in public from time to time until the end of her life. Brahms always sent his latest compositions for her to play over on the piano, and she sent him long and detailed observations and criticisms.

In 1878, Clara settled in Frankfort, her last home, where

she had been appointed a professor at the Hoch Conservatory. Her daughters Marie and Eugenie, both excellent pianists, served as her assistants. These daughters, who remained unmarried, were their mother's "guardian angels," as she often called them to Brahms. During these years in Frankfort, she gave a great deal of time and effort to preparing an edition of the complete piano works of Robert Schumann. Brahms was closely associated with her in this enterprise. One of her outstanding pupils during her last years was Carl Friedberg, a superb artist who for many years was head of the piano department at the Juilliard School in New York.

After Clara's death in Frankfort, on May 20, 1896, Marie Schumann, writing to a friend about a performance her mother had given for her pupils only a few months before, said that "she played with wonderful power and freshness, as also with her own peculiar rhythm."

Brahms died less than a year after Clara, in Vienna on April 3, 1897. It was said that his last illness was brought on by a chill he had caught at Clara's funeral. The tradition that he composed one of his last masterpieces, the *Vier ernste Gesänge*, op. 121, after Clara's death is not true. However, he did compose the songs just a few days before she died, when his thoughts were with her in her last illness and when he was seeking to reconcile himself to the inevitability of her death and his own.

There were during this century several other women pianists of great accomplishment, including Florence May, a pupil of Brahms; Ilona Eibenschütz, Clara's pupil; Fanny Davies, also Clara's pupil; and Sophie Metner, a Liszt pupil. But there was only one Clara Schumann, a fact that was realized by many of the hundreds who followed her cortège through the streets of Frankfort and Bonn. That cortège was headed by Brahms, one of the two great masters of music who had loved her and whom she had served so well.

～12～

Louis Moreau Gottschalk

1829=1869

A NATIVE of New Orleans, where he was born on May 8, 1829, Louis Moreau Gottschalk was the first American to gain international fame as a musician. The son of a cultivated English-born stockbroker who could speak eight languages and a Creole mother who was a good amateur singer, he began life with many advantages. At the age of three, he astonished his parents by reproducing on the pianoforte an aria his mother had been singing. At seven, he substituted in an emergency for the organist during Mass at the Cathedral of St. Louis in New Orleans. He played at his first concert when he was ten, after which his teachers for piano and violin told his father that there was nothing more they could teach him. The family reluctantly agreed to send their talented child to Paris for further study. Before his departure, in April, 1842, he gave a farewell concert that was attended by all of New Orleans society. The twelve-year-old prodigy was showered with bouquets and laurel wreaths, an experience that was to become familiar to him but which, though he always enjoyed it, never turned his head.

Since New Orleans was largely French by tradition, it was

logical for Gottschalk's parents to send him to Paris. As in Europe, the public taste in music in America was at that time overwhelmingly in favor of opera. Touring French and Italian troupes had begun to perform in New Orleans as early as 1791 and the elegant opera house, the Théâtre d'Orléans, where so many French operas had their American premières, was built in 1813. Although there were American pianoforte manufacturers in the north (the first, John Behrent, set up shop in Philadelphia in 1775), most of the instruments brought to New Orleans came by ship from France.

Gottschalk went to Paris alone and remained there, boarding with a family, for five years before he was joined by his mother and six brothers and sisters. His first piano teacher in Paris was Charles Hallé who, though he later became a famous pianist and conductor and founded the Hallé Orchestra of Manchester in England, was not, apparently, a very good teacher. It was Hallé who helped bring about a new vogue for "serious" piano music in London when, in 1848, he played Beethoven's Sonata op.31, no.3 at a concert of the Musical Union. Although earlier pianists had tried to interest the public in Beethoven's piano music, it was this performance by Hallé that apparently affected the public like a revelation.

After deciding that Hallé was not a satisfactory teacher, young Gottschalk's Paris guardians selected as successor Camille Stamaty, a pupil of Friedrich Kalkbrenner, a prominent virtuoso of the previous generation who had adopted the Logier system. Stamaty, who later taught the French pianist and composer Camille Saint-Saëns, turned out to be an excellent teacher for Gottschalk. As was the custom in those days, Gottschalk was introduced to the public not at a public concert but in various salons of the aristocracy, where he quickly gained a reputation. His first real concert appearance, though a non-paying one, was in April, 1845, at the Salle Pleyel, which had opened in 1830 with a concert at which Kalkbrenner was the star attraction. It was at this concert that Gottschalk performed Chopin's E Minor Concerto in the presence of the composer, who afterwards told him that he was destined to become "the king of pianists." He also performed difficult transcriptions by Thalberg and Liszt. His success was immediate and tremendous. The fact that he was an American, though more French than anything else, since he was from Louisiana, gave him a kind of exotic *cachet* for the Parisians. His triumph in Paris at the age of seventeen less one month was a kind of vindication for him, since he had applied for admission to the Paris Conservatoire and been refused by the head of the piano department, with the words "Americans are not musicians, they build railroads."

The poet Heinrich Heine, writing about musicians in Paris at this period, said that the city "serves them as a kind of billboard on which their fame may be read in enormous letters." Pianists were all the rage; and the piano was undergoing many changes. Between 1825 and 1851, almost two thousand patents pertaining to the piano were issued. These included various systems for stringing, maintaining tension, and increasing resonance, as well as various types of sounding boards. By the year 1868, there were in Paris an estimated twenty thousand people making all or part of their living by teaching the piano. When it came to giving a concert for which an admission was charged, however, the prudent pianist went first to the provinces. Gottschalk, following the example of two of his most celebrated predecessors, Liszt and Thalberg, gave his first commercial concert in the small city of Sedan. He then returned to the Salle Pleyel and gave a concert at which he played some of his own compositions, including his *Bamboula*, a dance piece based on a Negro theme that was to become greatly popular. It was after this concert that Thalberg, the nearest rival to Liszt, said to Gottschalk, "Young man, I predict for you a future such as few men have yet seen."

Though full of energy and determination, Gottschalk was physically frail and often suffered prolonged illnesses, during which he composed many of his unique piano works, such as *Danse Ossianique* and *Bananier*. He made an arrangement with a French publisher and in the future, both in France and America, could always count on a certain income from his published compositions. His big best seller was *The Last Hope*, which for a while in America threatened to equal the popularity of *The Maiden's Prayer*, an innocuous piece by Thekla Barderzewska that, after its publication in 1860, swept the New World, as Gottschalk put it, "like a plague."

Gottschalk's French career continued sporadically but triumphantly until 1851. He appeared in many of the French provincial cities and in Switzerland, where, at Geneva, the celebrated incident of his abduction by a young girl took place. Like many modern performers, he had a great following among young girls who crowded around him at stage doors. That night in Geneva, he was in poor health and so was unable to offer much resistance when a strapping Swiss maiden threw a cloak around him and carried him away. The incident was reported in the papers, and Gottschalk thought it best to leave town the next day.

After a Paris concert in April, 1851, the composer Berlioz wrote in the *Journal des Débats* that: "Mr. Gottschalk is one of the very small number of those who possess all the different elements of the sovereign power of the pianist, all the different elements which environ him with an irresistible prestige." Adolphe Adam, the composer of *Giselle* and *Cantique de Noël,* wrote that: "Mr. Gottschalk has all the grace and charm of Chopin, with more decided character; less magisterial than Thalberg, he has, perhaps, more warmth; less severe than Prudent, he has more grace and elegance." Émile Prudent was a popular player of the time, a follower of Thalberg and one of his rivals.

In 1851, Gottschalk answered a summons from the Queen of Spain and spent two years in her country. He enjoyed great favor at court and was received ecstatically every time he played in public. We learn from contemporary accounts that he usually played his own pieces, which were short and directly appealing, and, when the audience was particularly appreciative, had to repeat all of them at least once and some of them as many as five times. However, he did occasionally perform works of Chopin, to which he took the liberty of attaching romantic titles, and sometimes played Beethoven sonatas, despite the fact that he considered him an inferior composer for the piano, though sublime as a symphonist. This rather startling opinion appears to have been based on the fact that the piano in Beethoven's day was not what it was in Gottschalk's. A pianist like Gottschalk, who exploited all the new resources of volume, color, and speed that had been developed for his instrument, must have felt inhibited in performances of the works of the classic composers. He left Europe too soon to be aware of the kind of pianism that was to be promoted by Clara Schumann and others, or at least to be aware that it was to win the public.

Gottschalk began in Paris and continued in Spain a practice he was to continue for the rest of his career, which was to give the receipts from a certain percentage of his performances to charity. He later estimated that he had donated more than $150,000 in this way. Though his popularity in Spain was almost universal, one man at least was disgruntled by it: the court pianist who, at Valladolid, slammed a carriage door on Gottschalk's hand. It might have been an accident, but Gottschalk did not think so. It took him three months to recover; but he said that when he had, he found that his hand was stronger than ever.

On June 13, 1852, at Madrid, Gottschalk gave a great concert at which he introduced a new piece, *The Siege of Saragossa*, for ten pianos. The audience was roused to transports of musical and patriotic fervor. A huge crowd followed him to his hotel and the bands of two regiments serenaded him with his own *Danse Ossianique*. The next day, the most famous matador of the time sent him his sword, a significant compliment that Gottschalk fully appreciated.

Gottschalk returned to Paris the next year, but only for three weeks, during which he gave several concerts and visited his family. He then embarked for New York, a voyage of twenty-one days. Devoted as he was to his family, he never returned to France and never saw them again. His father, however, met him in New York, where Gottschalk gave his first concert in the ballroom of Niblo's Theater on February 11th. Six days later, he performed in the theater itself. These concerts resulted in a loss to himself of $2400. Even so, when he received an offer from P. T. Barnum to tour the country under his management, as the singer Jenny Lind had done a few years before, he was persuaded by his father to refuse.

Musical life in New York had been slower to develop than in Boston, Charleston, and New Orleans; but it had begun to come into its own by the time Gottschalk arrived there. The performances by Manuel García's company at the Park Theater in 1825 had established a taste for opera, and concerts of the New York Philharmonic, begun at the Apollo Rooms on Lower Broadway on December 7, 1842, now were being given regularly. In the year 1829, twenty-five hundred pianofortes were imported to the United States, of which those of Clementi & Co. were the most popular. Of American pianoforte makers, Dodds and Claus was established in New York in 1791 and Appleton, Hoyts, and Babcock in Boston in 1813. In 1800, John Isaac Hawkins invented what he called a "portable grand," which was admired by Thomas Jefferson. It was actually an upright of five and a half octaves with a metal frame for the sounding board and braced by iron bars. In 1825, Alpheus Babcock was granted a patent for a square piano with complete iron frame. It was manufactured in Philadelphia but never became prevalent. The great firm of Steinway, founded by Henry E. Steinweg began in 1853 on Varick Street in New York. Wilhelm Knabe established his firm in Baltimore four years later. The Boston firm of Chickering established in 1823 by Jonas Chickering, an apprentice to Alpheus Babcock, led the field in these days. They had secured a patent for an improved metal-frame square in 1840 and in ten years were selling a thousand instruments a year. In 1843, they introduced a grand with a one-piece metal frame.

Before the arrival of Gottschalk, New York had received visits from only a few international virtuosos. The first, who came during the 1830's, was Daniel Schlesinger, a pupil of Ferdinand Ries and Ignaz Moscheles. He died suddenly in New York after a concert at the City Hotel on February 4, 1839. In 1845, Leopold de Meyer, a pupil of Czerny who was know as "the sledgehammer pianist," gave an American tour, playing in sixty concerts and traveling as far west as St. Louis. He brought with him his own two Érard pianos. Henri Herz, who manufactured his own piano, brought one with him for his American tour in 1846, but soon was persuaded to use the Chickering, which he chose over all its competitors. Gottschalk brought his own Pleyel with him; and when Thalberg arrived in 1856 for his American tour, he had seven Érard grands in his luggage. Thalberg and Gottschalk, who were both touring mightily, finally met for a joint concert in Albany on January 27, 1857.

Though Gottschalk was the first American pianist of international celebrity, there were a few others of local importance, particularly Richard Hoffman, English-born but an American resident, who performed with Gottschalk and was much admired by him, and William Mason, a pupil of Liszt and son of the well-known hymn composer, Lowell Mason, who introduced the late sonatas of Beethoven in New York in 1854.

In October of that year, Gottschalk received the news of his father's death just before a concert in Boston. He gave the concert and was very well received. Boston's musical taste was well in advance of the time. The Mendelssohn Quintette Club, founded in 1849, was gaining acceptance for the chamber music of Mozart, Beethoven, Mendelssohn, and Schubert, much of which they introduced to the American public. The first public performance on the pianoforte in America had been given at Boston in March, 1771.

After returning in triumph to New Orleans, where he was

presented with a gold medal to go with his Spanish decorations, Gottschalk went to Cuba and then back to New York, where he played in eighty concerts during the season of 1855-56. The sudden death of his mother in Paris probably contributed to the restlessness that caused him to go on a tour of Cuba and Puetro Rico in company with the fourteen-year-old soprano, Adelina Patti, who was to become the most popular singer of her time. In Havana, he gave a concert that he described in his remarkable *Notes of a Pianist* as follows: "I set to work and composed, on some Spanish verses written for me by a Havanese poet, an opera in one act, entitled *Fête Champêtre Cubaine.* Then I composed a Triumphal Hymn and a grand march. My orchestra consisted of six hundred and fifty performers—eighty-seven choristers, fifteen solo singers, fifty drums and eighty trumpets—that is to say, nearly nine hundred persons bellowing and blowing to see who could scream the loudest."

Though he makes no mention of it in his memoirs, Gottschalk supposedly changed his style to suit Americans, that is, to suit the ladies, who predominated at his concerts. He featured more sentimental works like his *Last Hope, The Dying Poet,* and *Mazurka sentimentale* in preference to the more rhythmic pieces of exotic flavor based on Negro themes that were so popular in France and Latin America.

Gottschalk spent the years between 1856 and 1862 wandering through the West Indies, giving concerts, as he wrote, "whenever I could find a piano." His reasons for staying so long away from the centers of musical life were probably implicit in these words that he wrote at Ponce, in Puerto Rico: "For myself, who from a sickly and nervous nature, have always had a propensity to melancholy, the stirring and noisy existence which the career of nomad virtuoso imposes on me, is that to which I have the greatest antipathy; thus, above all, I have enjoyed at Plazuela what I have been deprived of for so many years, the first of all joys, not having to give a concert—that is to say, not being obliged, at a fixed hour, to bestow a certain quantity of inspiration for the price of a few dollars, but to find oneself in the home-life of a family; that is to say, to have the heart warmed by the contact of good and amiable people, and to forget the thousand and one jealousies and miseries to which the talented artist is exposed."

We know from the notes that he began to write at this time how dearly he paid for the lazy years in the West Indies when he returned to New York and resumed touring. The tours that he gave during the next five years would have broken the spirit and probably the health of the most robust of modern virtuosos. And yet, we find in Gottschalk's *Notes of a Pianist* very few complaints. Instead, we discover a hardheaded, generous, civilized man capable of the greatest good humor and tolerance, completely undeceived about himself and his calling, and capable of the most acute observation. A Catholic and a Southerner, he toured throughout the American North during the Civil War years and, though he felt a certain detached sympathy for the Confederacy, was a convinced abolitionist who had freed his own slaves immediately upon the death of his father. This is what he wrote after playing in Washington before the President and his wife: "Mrs. Lincoln has a very ordinary countenance. Lincoln is remarkably ugly, but has an intelligent air, and his eyes have a remarkable expression of goodness and mildness. After an encore I played my fantasia, *L'Union*, in the midst of great enthusiasm. Lincoln does not wear gloves. I played very badly, and was furious against myself, which, however, did not prevent many of my friends from coming to congratulate me on my success. One of them who was present at the first concert (at which, bye-the-bye, I played very well) said to me, 'Well and good, you are in the vein tonight, for at the first concert one saw that you were badly prepared.'" Another typical entry reads: "It is remarkable that almost all the Russians who are in America are Counts, just as almost all the musicians who abound in the United States are nephews of Spohr and Mendelssohn."

Toward the end of his American travels, Gottschalk estimated that he had traveled by railroad some eighty thousand miles and given eight thousand concerts (including those in Europe and the West Indies). He had also by then composed almost three hundred pieces of one kind or another. During these strenuous travels, he was accompanied by a "concert troupe," which at various times included Carlo Patti, a violinist, Carlotta Patti, a singer, and Amalia Patti, a pianist. These were the brother and sisters of the famous Adelina. One of Gottschalk's diary entries, written at Sandusky, Ohio, in 1862, reads: "The applause here consists of whistling, which frightened Patti very much."

Gottschalk always had transported with him two seven-and-a-half octave pianos specially constructed for him by Chickering, which he called his "mastadons." In 1864, he wrote: "Steinway and Chickering, Guelphs and Ghibbelines of the musicians, are divided into two factions—the Germans are for Steinway." There were at this time at least a dozen companies manufacturing pianos in the United States. The Steinway piano, which eventually was to gain the ascendency, first came into prominence on February 11, 1860, when it was played by a pianist named Sebastian Bach Mills in a performance of the Moscheles G Minor Concerto with the New York Philharmonic. Four years later, while meditating upon pianists and pianos, Gottschalk wrote: "Érard's, whose tone is robust, strong, heroic, slightly metallic, is adapted exclusively to the powerful action of Liszt. Pleyel's, less sonorous but poetical and, so to speak, languishing and feminine, corresponds to the elegiac style and frail organization of Chopin. There are many excellent makers in America, and my opinion is that ours are equal to the best pianos of Europe. I play Chickering's, not because all others are bad, but because I like their tone, fine and delicate, tender and poetic, because I can obtain, in the modifications of their sound, tints more varied than those of other instruments. The sound is in the execution of the pianist what colors are in painting."

As he traveled from New York to St. Louis to Norfolk to

Montreal, not once but many times, playing in every possible small town along the way, Gottschalk noted in his diary
that the audiences varied from large to small and from ecstatic to indifferent. He worked hard to please but was not
unduly put out when he failed to do so. He tried to concentrate on the amusing aspects of his occasional failures and
maintained his philosophic good humor despite the many
and persistent hardships of constant travel. The newspapers,
which usually praised him but sometimes reviled him, several times amused him by publishing reports of his death or
marriage. He never did marry, though he was not unsuscep-
tible to feminine charms. He tells us in his memoirs that he
never played wrong notes except when pretty girls were in
the front row.

In 1865, Gottschalk sailed from New York to California.
He played to great enthusiasm in the major towns there and,
usually, to polite but unresponsive audiences in the frontier
towns of the Nevada Territory. Just before one San Francisco concert, at which he was to perform in an arrangement
for ten pianos of the March from Wagner's *Tannhäuser,* he
learned that one of the professionals he had hired for the
occasion was ill. Fearing to antagonize the audience by producing nine instead of ten pianists, as had been advertised,
he accepted the services of a wealthy and influential amateur. Upon discovering that the young man in question was a
hopelessly bad player, he had the action removed from his
piano. The concert proceeded with the untalented amateur
showing off happily at a silent keyboard. Ten pianists playing one piece was a feat the public enjoyed; but it was not
really a novelty. In Philadelphia in 1846, Henri Herz had
played a piece with thirty-nine other pianists at a concert
that still showed a profit.

The last years of Gottschalk's life were passed in South
America, where he got caught in two revolutions, of which
he gives most interesting accounts in his *Notes.* More honors
were heaped upon him in Buenos Aires and Rio de Janeiro.
But the plague of cholera, which had been devastating Brazil

and her neighboring countries, struck him down. He collapsed during a concert in Rio, losing consciousness as he was playing one of his own pieces that had the ironic and, in the circumstances, sinister title of *Morte*. He died at Tijuca, near Rio, on December 18, 1869. His last composition, which was to become his most familiar to us today, the *Grand Tarantella* for piano and orchestra, was left unfinished at his death. This is the work that George Balanchine used for one of the most popular ballets currently in the repertory of the New York City Ballet.

We are beginning to rediscover Gottschalk now, not only as a composer of naïve but delightful music, but as a writer of uncommon excellence, whose observations of life on the two American continents during the crucial years of the Civil War are invaluable.

It was the famous French poet and critic, Théophile Gautier, who said in writing of Gottschalk: "Among our popular pianists today there are but few who have known how to create for themselves an incontestable individuality. . . . It is then more difficult than one might think to depart from the beaten track, and to have his own tent placed alongside those of the masters. If Mr. Gottschalk has been able, although still young, to acquire this individuality, it is perhaps owing to the fact that, after having formed his talent by solid studies, he has left it to wander carelessly in the fragrant savannas of his country, from which he has brought back to us the colors and perfumes."

~13~

Anton Rubinstein

1829-1894

"LISZT was an eagle, Rubinstein a lion." So wrote Camille Saint-Saëns, the intimate friend of Rubinstein who never rivalled him as a pianist but, in the judgment of posterity, excelled him as a composer. To the average person today, Rubinstein's name is hardly a familiar one, except in Russia, where it is still venerated. And yet, the man who is remembered now almost exclusively for two or three of his minor salon pieces was probably the most famous virtuoso of his time, the true successor of Liszt and the spiritual predecessor of half the great pianists of the twentieth century.

Rubinstein's story is one of tremendous labors, enormous successes, and gigantic failures. He knew many hardships and suffered many griefs. From a very early age, he was dedicated to professionalism in music and did as much as any man of his time to rescue it from the domination of amateurs. His mother, Kaleria Rubinstein, German-born and well-trained in music, instilled in him and in his brilliant brother, Nicholas, a love and respect for music and the habit of hard work. She was above all else a practical woman and a determined one.

Anton was born on November 28, 1829, at Vichvatinez in Bessarabia, a province of Southwestern Russia. His parents were farm people, members of a large clan of Rubinsteins.

In 1831, some sixty members of the clan made a two weeks' journey to Berdichev to undergo Christian baptism, since the strictures of Czar Nicholas I against the Jewish people, which included conscription and double taxes, could only be avoided in this way. Though baptism gave the Rubinsteins rights as citizens, it did not free them from prejudice and social discrimination.

In 1834, when Anton was five, three Rubinstein brothers and their families migrated to Moscow, making the long journey in wagons. Anton's father, Gregor, set up as a pencil manufacturer and for a while prospered. The family acquired a square piano, and Anton started lessons with his mother. Soon, it was apparent that his extraordinary gifts required more advanced training than Kaleria could give. Through friends, a new teacher was found, one who had gained sudden fame locally through one of his pupils. This new teacher was Alexander Ivanovich Villoing. It was he whom Rubinstein acknowledged as his only teacher. So great was Villoing's conviction about the boy's talent that he dedicated himself completely to guiding him and his career and, to a large extent, did so at his own expense. Villoing had influential connections among the ruling aristocracy and was able, when Anton was ten, to arrange for him to make his debut at an open-air concert in Moscow's Petrovsky Park. The concert took place on July 11, 1839. Young Rubinstein played with the orchestra in one movement from a concerto by Hummel and then performed alone the Fantasia from *Moisè* by Thalberg (the same piece that Thalberg had played in his competition with Liszt in 1837), pieces by John Field and Adolf Henselt, and, to finish, the *Galop chromatique* of Liszt.

Though prodigies had abounded in the days of Mozart, who was the most prodigious of them all, they later went out of fashion with the public for about fifty years. However, they had, since Liszt's first appearances, become a vogue again. Rubinstein's parents, after the success of his first concert, wanted to avoid exploiting him. So they sent him to

Paris with Villoing to have him trained at the Conservatoire. Cherubini, the director of the Conservatoire, who had refused admission to Liszt, did the same to Rubinstein. He would not even listen to him play. Villoing decided to take matters into his own hands and began to promote his pupil among the influential musicians and aristocrats with whom he had contact. He arranged for the boy to play for small gatherings in the showrooms of both Pleyel and Érard. After months of plotting and planning, Villoing had the satisfaction of receiving an invitation for his pupil to appear at a gala concert with the young violinist, Henri Vieuxtemps. The brilliant audience included Liszt, Chopin, Giocomo Meyerbeer, and the pianists Kalkrenner and de Meyer. Rubinstein created a sensation and Liszt proclaimed "on these shoulders my mantle will fall." Chopin invited the boy to his studio and played for him. Later, Liszt, becoming alarmed at the attention the boy was receiving, told Villoing: "Take him to Germany and have him taught to write a fugue." Villoing, knowing that this was the kind of advice that Rubinstein's mother would want him to listen to, agreed. But the lure was too great, and after Rubinstein had played in Amsterdam before the Queen of Holland and the Grand Duke Konstantin, son of the Czar, Villoing succumbed. Rubinstein was in demand, and, in the next two years, appeared in Vienna, Budapest, Cologne, Leipzig, Berlin, Hamburg, and London. His London debut in a concert at the Hanover Square Rooms in May, 1842, was sponsored by Ignaz Moscheles and Felix Mendelssohn. Though summoned to play for Queen Victoria, Rubinstein was unable to win immediate acceptance in London. He did not play there again for fifteen years and always considered English audiences the most difficult. They preferred, during these Victorian times, the less spectacular and more severe musicianship of the respectable Clara Schumann. At the time of his London debut, however, Moscheles and Thalberg were the favorite pianists. Villoing had expected that Moscheles would arrange for Rubinstein to play with the Philharmonic Society. The fact that he did not was probably due more to Moscheles' fear of Villoing as a potential rival teacher than the fear of a twelve-year-old boy as a rival pianist.

After further appearances in Norway, Sweden, Cologne, Vienna, Breslau (where he remained for some time and composed his first piano piece, *Ondine*), Rubinstein returned to Russia. He performed in Warsaw (then a Russian city) and, on March 20, 1843, made his debut in the presence of the Czar and Czarina in St. Petersburg, playing with the Philharmonic Society in a concerto by Villoing. He was invited to the Czar's palace and showered with gifts. But his mother was uneasy. She knew that at fourteen he was growing out of the prodigy class and was worried about his lack of training in other aspects of music. So, in the following year, she took him to Berlin for study. Her daughter Luba and her younger son Nicholas went with them.

In Berlin, acting on the advice of Meyerbeer and Mendelssohn, then the two most prominent musicians of that city, Kaleria Rubinstein persuaded the most erudite of teachers, Siegfried Dehn, to accept Anton and Nicholas as pupils. However, after less than two years, Gregor Rubinstein died, leaving his family bankrupt. Kaleria went back to Moscow with Luba and Nicholas, leaving Anton behind. She was forced to become a teacher in a girl's seminary and Nicholas, aged eleven, went on tour as a prodigy in Russia. Villoing went with him.

The next few years were the hardest of Anton Rubinstein's life. He had to make his own way and was determined to do so. He left Berlin for Vienna, where he had been particularly acclaimed as a prodigy. He called on Liszt but was coldly received. The prodigy was no more and the awkward youth did not know how to make himself appealing to the man who was the greatest star of the musical world. It soon became obvious to Rubinstein that nobody wanted him now, and he scraped up a living by giving lessons whenever he could. He finally managed to save enough money to finance a concert; but it was a total failure. He was hissed. Then, he and his friend Heindle, a flautist, decided to go to America. They made some money giving concerts in provincial Hungarian towns and set off for Berlin, en route to the New World. They arrived in Berlin just in time to attend Mendelssohn's funeral. Rubinstein went to call on his teacher, Dehn, who somehow managed to persuade him that going to America was not a good idea. This was the year 1848, which was one of revolutionary uprisings in Germany and France. There were barricades in the streets of Paris and Berlin. Heindle, the flautist, was killed by a sniper while crossing a street. Rubinstein, sensing that the world was changing rapidly and that his own country could not remain immune, decided to go home.

He was not well received in St. Petersburg. Anti-Semitic prejudice was on the rise again. Nobody knew or cared who Rubinstein was, and he suddenly found himself in danger of arrest because he lacked a passport. Influential friends finally intervened, but he had his way to make all over again in Russia. He gave lessons and set about wooing the aristocrats. The Czar's official pianist, Adolf Henselt, helped, and so did Henri Vieuxtemps, who came to Russia on tour and played with Rubinstein in concerts, one of which was a particularly distinguished court affair. Slowly, Rubinstein impressed himself upon the Petersburg public, which was the court and the aristocracy. Nicholas I was musical, but to him musicians were suspect as possible revolutionaries. He maintained a strict and unprogressive court. However, his sister-in-law, the Grand Duchess Helena Pavlovna, who was born a Princess of Würtemburg, was a secret liberal and a devoted if restricted patron of music. She recognized Rubinstein's genius and shared with him his opinions about the state of music in Russia. They became friends and, in 1852, she appointed him her Master of Music.

For two years, Rubinstein lived in the Grand Duchess Helena's Petersburg Palace and at her summer villa on Kammenoy Island, where he composed his two most famous piano pieces, the *Kammenoy Ostrov,* which has become a

A Cristofori pianoforte, built about 1720 (THE METROPOLITAN MUSEUM OF
ART, THE CROSBY BROWN COLLECTION OF MUSICAL INSTRUMENTS, 1889)

Thomas Gainsborough's portrait of Johann Christian Bach

Muzio Clementi (THE BETTMANN ARCHIVE)

LEFT TO RIGHT: *An artist; Hector Berlioz, the composer; Karl Czerny, Liszt's teacher; Franz Liszt at the piano; Hans Wilhelm Ernst, the violinist* (THE BETTMANN ARCHIVE)

Clara and Robert Schumann (THE BETTMANN ARCHIVE)

Louis Moreau Gottschalk (THE BETTMANN ARCHIVE)

Teresa Carreño (THE BETTMANN ARCHIVE)

Ferruccio Busoni (THE BETTMANN ARCHIVE)

kind of traditional Easter hymn, and the *Melody in F,* which for years to come was to be one of the most popular of salon pieces. He had by this time also composed his first opera, *Dmitri Donskoy,* two concertos, and a symphony. It was after the unsuccessful production of *Dmitri Donskoy* in Petersburg in 1852 that the Grand Duchess Helena gave him his appointment, for she was inspired by it to conceive of a new kind of nationalistic Russian opera, a dream in which Rubinstein shared. But, for all his heroic efforts, he was to compose only one opera out of many that managed to hold the stage.

The friendship of the Grand Duchess was one of the most meaningful in Rubinstein's life. Her influence and patronage were of crucial importance, not only to his career, but to the whole future of musical life in Russia. However, the position Rubinstein held as her music master, though it gave him security and threw him into contact with the influential aristocracy, provided him with little scope. So, in 1854, he resigned and left Russia to pursue his virtuoso's career. His successor in the Grand Duchess' household was Theodor Leschetizky, one of Rubinstein's lifelong friends, a pupil of Czerny who was to become the most celebrated piano teacher in Europe.

Rubinstein knew that the best way to promote himself as a pianist outside Russia was to win the approval of Liszt. So he went to Weimar, where the great man was living, and presented himself. Liszt was an easy captive, for Rubinstein had confidence now and had matured into a virtuoso who, it was soon to become apparent, had no rival except the master of Weimar himself. Liszt, ever generous to musicians of talent, gave Rubinstein what he really wanted, which was encouragement as a composer as well as a pianist. Performances of Rubinstein's music were given at Weimar, and Liszt, who had only to say the word, arranged for some of it to be published. Rubinstein was happy at Weimar, though he was indifferent to the aesthetic arguments about classicism versus the "new music" of Liszt and Wagner that so much concerned Liszt and his followers. He secretly held a low opinion of Liszt's more ambitious compositions and cordially disliked the music of both Wagner and Brahms. He was, as a composer, a reactionary, which was one reason why his music never had as much success as he thought it should. But he was over-prolific and too undisciplined a composer ever to create a real masterpiece. He lacked self-criticism as a composer as much as he possessed it as a pianist. But he cared desperately and worked unremittingly. Some of his music had power and effect and enjoyed limited popularity in his time. Certainly, he had a gift for melody. But he was trying to compose like Mendelssohn at a time when the public taste was being molded by Wagner and Brahms. It must have been a source of puzzlement to him that in his own country the finest and most lasting music was composed by Tchaikovsky, whom he did not consider a really serious musician.

The death of Nicholas I in 1855 and the coronation of the new Czar, Alexander II, in the next August caused Rubinstein to return to Russia briefly. After the ceremonies and festivities attending the coronation, he went to the French Riviera with the Grand Duchess Helena and some of her friends. The Grand Duchess had come into her own, for the new Czar adored her, respected her, and took council from her. Together, they were plotting the historic move that Alexander II made in February, 1861, when he emancipated the Russian serfs. This was done just as the United States was plunging into its great struggle over the abolition of slavery.

Rubinstein conquered Paris, where at that time musical reputations were made or broken, in April, 1857. The times were ripe for a virtuoso of his caliber, for Chopin was dead, Moscheles and Liszt had retired, and Thalberg and Gottschalk were touring in America. Rubinstein was to be the almost unchallenged champion of pianists for the next thirty years. But he was never content with that. He composed prodigiously and toiled constantly at the piano to improve his playing and to achieve the same sort of piercing sweetness of tone that had so impressed him when, years ago as a boy in Paris, he first heard the famous Italian tenor, Giovanni Battista Rubini. It was at this time that he began the series of Biblical opera-oratorios that was to occupy him for the rest of his life. The first was *Paradise Lost,* which was based not on the Bible but on Milton. It was produced by Liszt at Weimar in 1858. This led to six others, none of them successful, and he was working on a seventh when he died. His only successful opera was not one of these but another, *The Demon,* produced in Petersburg in 1875. It is still in the repertory of Russian opera houses. It has been suggested that the sacred operas that were so dear to his heart were composed to expiate his family's renunciation of Judaism, while another theory holds that they constituted Rubinstein's answer to Wagner's mythological operas.

Rubinstein returned to Russia again in 1859, turning his back for the time being on the career of international virtuoso for the sake of the plan that he and the Grand Duchess Helena had evolved for the advancement of music in Russia. That November he played in Petersburg at the first concert of the Musical Society, which he had formed. Professional classes then were begun in the Grand Duchess' palace. The Petersburg Conservatory, the dream of Rubinstein's life, was inaugurated in October, 1861, under the patronage of the Czar, who had been persuaded by the Grand Duchess. Rubinstein had done his work well, securing for his faculty such distinguished musicians as the pianist Theodor Leschetizky, the violinist Henri Wieniawski, the cellist Karl Davidov, the pianist Alexander Dreyschock, and the theorist and composer, Nicolai Zaremba.

Nicholas Rubinstein founded a branch of the Musical Society in Moscow in 1860 and six years later became director of the Moscow Conservatory, modeled on his brother's Petersburg original. Though the conservatory system, once established, was immediately successful in Russia, there was opposition to it from musicians of a more revolutionary persuasion who thought that it was not sufficiently nationalistic and was too much dominated by foreigners and aristocrats. The most persistent and vitriolic of the opponents was the composer Mili Balakirev, leader of the Slavophile group known as "The Five" that did succeed in revolutionizing Russian music, particularly through the works of its two most creative members, Modest Moussorgsky and Nikolai Rimski-Korsakov. The other members of "The Five" were César Cui and Alexander Borodin. Though all of the five were greatly talented, they were amateurs, largely untrained in music. For this Rubinstein despised them, though he appears to have had friendly personal relations with them. Rimski-Korsakov eventually recognized his limitations, entered the conservatory, and ultimately became its director and greatest teacher. Pëtr Ilich Tchaikovsky, Russia's greatest composer, entered the Petersburg Conservatory as a pupil of Zaremba in 1861 and was a member of Rubinstein's class in instrumentation. Ironically, it was Nicholas Rubinstein, second as a pianist only to his brother, who crushed Tchaikovsky by refusing to play his B flat Concerto, which is now probably the most popular of all piano concertos. He later relented, however, and played it with great success on a European concert tour.

In 1867, Rubinstein, thinking that his work at the conservatory was done, resigned. He was succeeded as director by Zaremba. His old enemy, Balakirev, succeeded him as director of the concerts of the Musical Society. Perhaps the fact that Rubinstein now had family responsibilities had much to do with his decision to resume his concert career. He had married the Princess Vera Alexandrovna Chekuanov in 1860. They had two sons and a daughter and lived in a luxurious villa near the Czar's summer palace at Peterhof. Their expenses were great. Rubinstein in his life made several fortunes and gave away several, to charity, students, friends. He was incredibly generous but ruthless, too, when it came to enforcing his musical standards and warring with amateurs. His capacity for work was incredible. He toured almost constantly, from one European city to another, always working to improve and extend his repertory, though it was already known to be the biggest repertory of any pianist of the time.

The famous American tour that Rubinstein gave began with a concert in New York at Steinway Hall on September 23, 1872. He played his own D Minor Concerto with the New York Philharmonic, and solos by Handel, Mozart, Beethoven, and Schubert. His effect on the American public was like nothing that had ever happened before. The only musicians to have so conquered it were Jenny Lind and the violinist Ole Bull. Rubinstein became legend in America in more ways than one. A monologue called *How Ruby Played* became a favorite recitation piece, both in vaudeville and in parlors, for years. Rubinstein's contract was for two hundred concerts at $200 each. He was sponsored by William Steinway and managed by Maurice Grau, who later was a manager of the Metropolitan Opera. The violinist Henri Wieniawski made the tour with him, getting only half as much money and half as much attention. Their friendship was severely strained as a result. Rubinstein composed a Fantasia on *Yankee Doodle,* which he played at his farewell concert. He gave the first solo recital in New York's history on January 13, 1873. Grau had predicted disaster, but it packed the house. So, at the end of his tour, Rubinstein gave six solo recitals in eight days in New York, exploring the whole of piano literature from Scarlatti to Mendelssohn and Rubinstein. His *Ocean* Symphony was performed by Theodore Thomas' Orchestra, much to Rubinstein's gratification.

In all, Rubinstein gave 215 concerts in America in 239 days. His contract stipulated that he be paid in gold and that he not be required to perform "at any establishments devoted to other than artistic purposes." Steinway Hall, seating 2500 people, had been opened in 1866. On April 25, 1873, Rubinstein appeared with two American pianists, Sebastian Bach Mills and William Mason, in a Bach concerto for three pianos with Theodore Thomas' Orchestra. As a result of Rubinstein's American tour, many people heard for the first time, at least in public, works of Bach, Beethoven, Chopin, and Schumann; for until then, pianists had performed either their own works or those by the more popular "lighter" composers. Though the works that Rubinstein played were now considered classics in Europe, they were not so in America, despite the efforts of musicians like William Mason, Theodore Thomas, and Sebastian Bach Mills and the regular concerts by the Philharmonic Society. Rubinstein created a taste not only for piano virtuosos but for the piano classics. His tour was followed, three years later, by another given by one of his nearest rivals, Hans von Bülow. It was von Bülow who first played the Tchaikovsky concerto after Nicholas Rubinstein rejected it and who introduced it to America in 1875.

After this American tour and the successful production in Petersburg of his opera *The Demon,* Rubinstein was made an hereditary nobleman by the Czar. He had, while playing in Boston, received the news of the death of the Grand Duchess Helena. When he received this new honor on returning to Russia, he suspected that it was the work of his old friend, the last of many things that she had done for him. As he always did when sorrow struck, he threw himself even more intensely into work, composing and always playing. He never gave up trying to compose a truly Russian opera, but his detractors said they were more German than anything else. Actually, he was never to achieve the kind of individual character in his music that is evident in the few operas that are truly Russian, those by Moussorgsky and Rimski-Korsakov, as well as the two by Tchaikovsky that are familiar to us today.

Although Rubinstein was a pianist on the grand scale, he enjoyed ensemble playing and often performed at chamber music concerts with such notable artists as Wieniawski, Vieuxtemps, Alfredo Piatti, and Leopold Auer. Auer became the most famous of all violin teachers, but he refused to play the Tchaikovsky violin concerto on the grounds that it was too difficult.

Rubinstein—whose physical resemblance to Beethoven was noted by many, including Liszt, who had known the great composer—often performed as many as eight of the master's sonatas at one concert. His greatest accomplishment as a pianist was his series of "historical concerts," as he called them. These were seven recitals in rapid succession, including the great piano works of all the important composers from Couperin to Tchaikovsky. Between 1885 and 1887, he gave this series in Petersburg, Moscow, Berlin, Vienna, Leipzig, Paris, and London. It was a pianistic feat that never has been equalled, except perhaps by another pianist of the same name, but no relation, Artur Rubinstein. The first program consisted of piano pieces by Byrd, Bull, Couperin, Rameau, Scarlatti, J.S. Bach, K.P.E. Bach, Haydn, and Mozart. The second program consisted of eight Beethoven Sonatas. The third program had major works by Schubert, Weber, and Mendelssohn. The fourth was all Schumann. The fifth consisted of pieces by Clementi, John Field, Hummel, Moscheles, Henselt, Thalberg, and Liszt. The sixth was all Chopin. The seventh began with Chopin and continued with Glinka, Balakirev, Cui, Rimski-Korsakov, Liadov, Tchaikovsky, and Nicholas and Anton Rubinstein.

Though Steinway had established a factory at Hamburg in 1880, the piano used by Rubinstein at the historical concerts was a Bechstein. Founded by Friedrich Bechstein, the Bechstein firm, established in 1856 in Berlin, had become the most successful in Europe.

In 1880, Nicholas Rubinstein died in Paris. Czar Alexander II was assassinated the same year. The new Czar, Alexander III, restored many autocratic and repressive measures. Anton Rubinstein resumed his directorship of the Petersburg Conservatory seven years later and remained until 1891. He gave a famous series of lecture-recitals at the conservatory, which made a profound impression on all who attended them. From contemporary accounts of his playing it is apparent that Rubinstein often played inaccurately but always with power and passion. He was referred to as "a volcanic eruption" and "a son of thunder." He was the opposite of von Bülow, who planned every note carefully and seldom changed his interpretations. Rubinstein's playing was spontaneous, variable, unpredictable. His effect on audiences was always magnetic. Though he was uncompromising in his musical idealism, his interpretations were highly personal and sometimes erratic. He did not change notes, or add them, as Liszt was accused of doing, but he hardly ever played notes twice the same way.

In 1889 his jubilee was celebrated in Petersburg. Many concerts and balls were given for he was by now a national hero, and to his students he was a god. His last appearance in Russia was in the Hall of the Nobility at a concert of his own music on January 14, 1894. The following April, he was persuaded to play for Leschetizky's students in Vienna. His last public appearance was in June at a concert in Stuttgart after the production there of his opera, *Christus*.

Brahms once described to Clara Schumann one of Rubinstein's works as "now insignificant, then atrocious, and anon having a touch of profundity." Clara answered that what Rubinstein "lacks above all is sacred seriousness." Rubinstein himself once said: "Genius is forgotten, but the worker, the true worker, can always make himself known to the world." This was certainly true of him. The consensus of history is that Rubinstein's music lacks genius, but the sheer force and persistence of his efforts impressed his contemporaries, and many of his works were popular in their time.

Just before his death, at his Peterhof villa on November 20, 1894, Rubinstein said: "All that I care that men shall remember me by is my conservatory." Certainly, the many brilliant pianists produced by that conservatory, all of whom, directly or indirectly, were influenced by Rubinstein, spread its fame throughout the world. The great virtuoso, Josef Hofmann, was one of the few pupils Rubinstein ever taught privately. Sergei Rachmaninoff, one of the greatest pianists of his time, was a student at the Moscow Conservatory, where he studied with Alexander Siloti, the most celebrated pupil of Nicholas Rubinstein. The prize that Anton Rubinstein established and which was given every five years until the Russian Revolution was won first by Rubinstein's pupil, Ossip Gabrilówitsch, and later by Josef Lhévinne. Both Gabrilówitsch and Lhévinne were among the most admired players of their generation.

Rubinstein died the day after Czar Alexander II was buried. The new Czar was the tragic Nicholas II. Rubinstein, who had some experience of revolution and revolutionaries, might not have cared for the new Russia that was created after the 1917 revolution. He, like Liszt, admired the institution of aristocracy and did not mind doing what was necessary to cultivate the favor of wealthy and powerful aristocrats. But the new Russia honors Rubinstein's bequest to it, which is his conservatory. It also honors some of his music and, in producing notable piano virtuosos of today like Emil Gilels, Sviatislav Richter, and Vladimir Ashkenazy, honors the tradition that he established.

~14~

Teresa Carreño

1853-1917

THE woman who became known as "the Valkyrie of the piano" was often and more aptly described as an Amazon, for she was not Nordic and blonde but Latin and dark. Her extraordinary gifts came to her naturally, for the Carreños of Venezuela were the leading musicians of that country for several generations. Though an amateur, Manuel Antonio Carreño, the father of Teresa, was a talented pianist and composer. In later years, after the success of his daughter, he became a much admired teacher and developed a method based on the techniques he had used in training her.

Born in the Venezulean capital of Caracas on December 22, 1853, Teresa Carreño was so obviously musical that it soon became evident that she belonged to the world and not merely to her troubled and unstable native country. She was only eight when her father took her to New York, where he thought to obtain for her more advanced teaching. But the impression she made on all who heard her play was so much more profound than is generally the case with prodigies that it was decided to present her to the public. The idol of the public at that time was Louis Moreau Gottschalk, who, when he heard her play, was so persuaded that he abandoned the prejudice he had formed against all prodigies. He endorsed her and even urged that she perform in concert. "She must be something great," he wrote, "and shall be." Because of his almost incessant touring, he was able to give Carreño only a few lessons, and she knew him for no more than a year. But he remained the inspiration and model of her early years.

Carreño's debut took place at Irving Hall in New York on November 25, 1862. She performed the *Rondo Brilliante* of Hummel, Thalberg's Fantasia on *Moisè*, a Nocturne by Doehler, and the *Jerusalem Fantasie* of Gottschalk. As usual at concerts in those days, other artists appeared on the program, including the young violinist Theodore Thomas, who soon was to become one of the most influential musicians in America.

Teresita, as everybody called her then, swept all before her. Pretty, charming, well-mannered, and, above all, incredibly adept for a child of eight, she was, at least at this stage, irresistible. She played three concerts a week in various eastern American cities and, in 1863, performed at the White House for President and Mrs. Lincoln, improvising, at Lincoln's request, on his favorite song, "Listen to the Mocking Bird." Fifty-five years later, she was to play at the White House again, this time for President Woodrow Wilson.

In 1864, Teresita went to Cuba, where she performed works of Chopin and Beethoven for the first time, and then returned with her family to Caracas. She was twelve when her father decided to take her to Paris, the real capital of the world in the minds of all South Americans. After her debut at the Salle Érard on May 14, 1866, she was established as the prodigy of the day. She played for Rossini and Liszt, both of whom were enchanted, and later met Anton Rubinstein, who gave her lessons at infrequent intervals. She always considered him her true guide and mentor. He adored her and called her his "sunshine." No doubt there was much that he taught her, though as a teacher he had no method and taught more by example than anything else.

Carreño's novelty as a prodigy wore off eventually and, like Rubinstein and Gottschalk before her, she had to make her way as a maturing artist, competing not with a small number of remarkable children but a large number of competent adults. She soon began doing what every struggling musician must do, which is to teach. One of her pupils in Paris was Liszt's daughter, Blondine Ollivier. Carreño also toured with various concert troupes, some of them better than others. For the rest of her life, hardly a year passed that did not find her touring far and wide. At first she was simply a passé prodigy, though generally she was singled out for praise by the critics when she played with the concert troupes. She discovered also that she could sing and for a while was more interested in an operatic career.

During one of her tours with a concert troupe, she was suddenly called upon to make an impromptu opera debut in Edinburgh, singing the very difficult role of Marguerite de Valois in Meyerbeer's *Les Huguenots*. This was in 1872 when Carreño was nineteen. She appeared under the name of the singer she was replacing, who got the credit for a good performance. The star of the evening, singing the role of Valentine, was Thérèse Tietjens, the greatest soprano of her time. With another concert troupe, Carreño often performed the Beethoven *Kreutzer* Sonata with the great violinist Joachim.

After her opera debut, Carreño went on an American tour with Carlotta Patti, the aging tenor Mario, once the tenor of all tenors, and a violinist named Émile Sauret. She and Sauret, who later became a celebrated artist, fell in love and were married in New York on July 13, 1872. Their daughter, Emilita, was born two years later. After another American tour, Carreño and Sauret separated, for they had conflicts both in private and on the concert platform. The cold, reserved French violinist and the hot-tempered but warmhearted South American pianist simply could not agree about anything. Later, Carreño was forced to consent to the adoption of Emilita by a German woman and, though she tried to do so, did not see this child again for more than thirty years.

Distressed by the sudden collapse of her marriage,

Carreño gave up concerts for a while and took up residence in Boston, where she studied singing. On February 25, 1876, she made her formal debut in opera as Zerlina in Mozart's *Don Giovanni*. Performances were given in New York and Boston. Tietjens was in the cast and the title role was sung by the young Italian baritone Giovanni Tagliapietra. Though her singing and acting were praised and a career in opera appeared to be possible, Carreño wisely decided that she was a better pianist than singer. A contract with the Weber piano company that provided a small fixed income in exchange for using their piano exclusively encouraged her to resume a concert career. Perhaps her chief motive for giving up singing professionally was her attachment to Giovanni Tagliapietra, who became her second husband. One singer in the family was enough. Though the marriage lasted twelve years and was blessed by three childern, the first of which died, it was not a happy one. Tagliapietra was a gambler and philanderer, an egotistical artist who received less attention from the public than his wife. She might have been glad to retire into domesticity but could not, for she rather than her husband was the steady support of the family. Between childbirths, she toured, often with Tagliapietra and also with other distinguished artists. On another tour with Leopold Damrosch and his orchestra, she performed the Grieg Concerto and had much to do with making that work popular in America. At this time she also began performing the works of her friend and pupil, Edward MacDowell. She continued to include his works in her programs for the rest of her life and was the first to perform the work that he dedicated to her, his D Minor Concerto, both in America and abroad. Her own composition, the *Teresita Waltz*, written in honor of her daughter soon after her birth, became one of her regular encores and in published form had a steady sale in America and Europe for many years.

In 1885, Carreño returned to Venezuela and was received as a national heroine. After so many years of third-class railroad travel and third-rate hotels, the adulation she received and the luxury with which she suddenly found herself surrounded must have been pleasing indeed. Since she was the grandniece of the South American liberator, Simón Bolivar, and a cousin of the then current Venezuelan president, as well as the most famous musician ever to come out of that country, it was not surprising that she was asked to return the next year, not merely as a pianist but as the organizer and director of an opera company. On returning to Europe, she left the details to Tagliapietra, thinking he would know better than she how to engage singers and make all the arrangements. However, when the Teresa Carreño Opera Company opened its season in Caracas, disaster followed disaster. The troupe became a focus for political controversy and combat and, for some reason, Tagliapietra was singled out for hostility on the part of the public. When the conductor defected because of threatened assaults by tomatoes and rotten eggs, Carreño took over, wielding the baton at performances of *La Favorita, La Sonnambula, Il Trovatore,* and *Lucia di Lammermoor.* This was her only experience as a conductor and her last visit to her native land. It also marked the end of her marriage to Tagliapietra.

In the year 1889, Carreño, taking stock of herself, decided that, though she had played in some 1650 concerts in eleven years, she was not satisfied with herself as a musician. She had always wanted to go to Germany, where, by this time, musical standards were the highest and critics the toughest. And she needed a radical change after the failure of her second marriage. A friend loaned her enough money to permit her to go abroad with her children and finance a new career. Her Berlin debut at the Singakademie on November 18 was the crucial appearance of her career. She played the Grieg Concerto with the Berlin Philharmonic and then performed alone in the *Symphonic Études* of Schumann and the *Polonaise Brilliante* of Weber-Liszt. Her kind of playing had seldom if ever been heard in Berlin and she feared she would not be liked. But she was a sensation. Critics compared her to Rubinstein and, while they pointed out her unconventional rubatos and other deviations from the letter of the law, were carried away by her range and temperament, by her masculine power and feminine subtlety. From that day on, Carreño was in the forefront of pianists. With Rubinstein in Russia, von Bülow now concentrating on conducting, and younger virtuosos not yet established, she was considered to have no rival except one, Eugen d'Albert, the Scottish-born pupil of Liszt who became the most famous of the master's disciples.

D'Albert and Carreño did not meet until 1891, after she had played in Russia, where she was reunited with Rubinstein. Grieg heard her perform his concerto in Leipzig on March 29, 1890, and said to her afterwards, "Madame, I did not know that my concerto was so beautiful." So, by the time she and d'Albert did meet, it was as equals and rivals. He was eleven years younger than she and a small, gnome-like man. She disliked him at first, but that soon changed, and he became her third husband. After five years and two children, both daughters, it was all over. Naturally, the marriage and eventual divorce of two such famous artists attracted much publicity. Carreño had thought that for the first time in her adult life she would be protected and supported by a man who was as strong as she was. But this turned out not to be the case. D'Albert was anything but generous. They tried giving two-piano concerts together, but their temperaments clashed. She performed his piano concerto over and over again, but the critics always praised her and not him. He wanted to compose operas and did, without much success until 1903, years after his marriage to Carreño, when his *Tiefland* was produced. That opera is still performed occasionally in Europe.

D'Albert was one of the great pianists of his time; but in later years he neglected his technique because of his intense activity as a composer, and when he was compelled to perform in order to make money, never was able to regain his old standard. He married six times. Once, when in London, he was introduced to a very famous actress who stared at him and then said, "Oh yes, d'Albert, you're the man who marries everybody."

Carreño, finding herself again the sole support of four children, resumed her strenuous seasons, touring constantly during the concert months and summering in the mountains. She played from fifty to seventy concerts a year and sometimes even more. She was always in demand for appearances with the best orchestras under the best conductors. She achieved new triumphs in the Beethoven *Emperor* Concerto, adjusting her style, so romantic in Chopin, to the more classical demands of this work. She began to teach in earnest, composed a string quartet that was generally admired, and tried to make musicians out of her children. In this, however, she was not successful. Her oldest daughter, Teresita, made her debut as T. C. Tagliapietra in 1901. She had brilliant gifts but was an undisciplined and temperamental girl. Her career was a fitful one, and she never lived up to her promise. Carreño's son, Giovanni Tagliapietra, had promise as a singer, but he suffered from the same faults as his sister and had his father's faults as well. Carreño, whatever her faults, had the most extraordinary discipline, performing according to her always heavy schedule whatever her mood, whatever her health, which was not always good, and whatever misfortunes pursued her.

Carreño returned to America as a major artist in 1897 under the auspices of the Knabe Piano Company. She performed first with the New York Philharmonic in the Rubinstein D Minor Concerto. She returned for tours in 1899, under Chickering auspices, in 1901 for Steinway, and in 1913 for the Everett Company. In addition, she gave a lengthy tour of Australia, New Zealand, and the United States in 1906-1907 and another to the United States, New Zealand, Australia, and South Africa from 1909 to 1911. In Europe, she always used the Bechstein piano. While touring in England, she performed with the young violin virtuoso, Mischa Elman, and in two piano recitals with Wilhelm Backhaus, who became one of the leading pianists of the twentieth century.

On June 30, 1902, Carreño married again, creating another scandal, for her fourth husband, Arturo Tagliapietra, was the brother of her second. However, this marriage was entirely successful and brought to Carreño in her last years the happiness she had never had. The war years were hard for her in many ways. Both her daughter Teresita and her son Giovanni were interned as suspected spies, she in Tunisia and he in Italy. Teresita spent three and a half months in prison and was for some time in danger of execution. Giovanni was in prison only for eighteen days. When her children finally were safe in neutral countries, Carreño gave up her longtime home in Berlin and went to America with her husband. Both her younger daughters married in Berlin after she left, little knowing that their mother never would return.

Carreño took up residence in New York, acquired a good many pupils, and performed in concert whenever possible. Her last appearance was in Havana on March 21, 1917. She had been stricken with an eye ailment that produced double vision, so she played with her eyes tightly shut. Her final illness was sudden and short. Her death in New York on June 12 was said to be due to the collapse of her nervous system after fifty-five years of unremitting strain and hard work. Her funeral was attended by many famous musicians; one of the honorary pallbearers was the most famous of all the pianists who came after her, Paderewski.

James Huneker, one of the best of all critics, once wrote about Carreño: "Her manner of playing for me has always seemed scarlet, as Rubinstein's was golden, and Joseffy's silver." (Rafael Joseffy, a pupil of Liszt and Taussig, became famous in America in 1897 and was a noted teacher.) There is no doubt that Carreño was the greatest woman pianist after Clara Schumann. She traveled further and longer than that distinguished artist and, even more than she, blazed the way for musicians of her sex. She has had few successors. In our times, the one who apparently comes nearest to her is the great Brazilian pianist, Guiomar Novaes. But comparisons are useless, for we have no real record of Carreño's playing except some music rolls she made during the early days of the vogue for player pianos, and those she disowned on the grounds that all that was characteristic in her playing was lost on them.

Venezuela, Carreño's native land, finally reclaimed her on February 15, 1938, when her ashes were returned to Caracas and a memorial concert, featuring compositions by her ancestors, was given. Her difficult but beloved daughter, Teresita, came from London to witness these last honors for her mother.

~15~

Ignace Jan Paderewski

1860=1941

DURING the last years of the nineteenth century and the early years of the twentieth, one pianist stood above all others in the public esteem. That was Paderewski. It appears to have been the man as much as the artist that captured people. Apparently, though many of his fellow artists criticized his playing severely, none of them could resist it or him. Many writers have told about the hush that descended on a gathering whenever he appeared and of the awe he inspired not only in audiences but in even his most formidable rivals. Today, we can only guess at the qualities that contributed to his magic. He was often described as "a prince among men." His appearance, which suggested both strength and poetry, his manner, which was aristocratic but without affectation, and his musicianship, which was highly individual, all had something to do with it. Through extraordinary circumstances, he became a symbol of nobility, not merely in music, but in politics and world affairs. Though it must at times have been difficult to function as a symbol, he did it as well as any man can and never failed in what was expected of him.

Paderewski was not a prodigy, though he probably could have been, and his destiny did not really manifest itself until he was almost thirty. Born on November 18, 1860, at Kurylówa in Poland, he composed his first piece at six and made one public appearance as a pianist when he was twelve, at the time when he entered the Warsaw Musical Institute. Except for a tour of smaller Russian cities with a violinist when he was seventeen, he remained a student until his graduation at eighteen. Then he was appointed an instructor in piano at the Warsaw Institute. His first piece to be published, the *Impromptu in F*, appeared the next year. His ambition at this time was concentrated on composing. In 1880, he married Antonia Korsak, who died giving birth to their son the following year. This tragedy led him to change his life. He left the Institute and went to Berlin to begin concentrated studies in counterpoint and orchestration.

It was not until 1884 that Paderewski began to consider a career as a pianist. In that year, he went to Vienna to become a pupil of Theodor Leschetizky with whom he coached intensively for three years. During this period, he spent part of his time teaching at the Strasbourg Conservatory and in summer vacations went to Zakopane in the Tatra mountains. His *Tatra Album* for piano was inspired by these surroundings and by the distinctive folk music of the people who live there.

Though the guidance and encouragement of Leschetizky must have been decisive in persuading Paderewski to take up the difficult career of a virtuoso, it was supposedly the famous Polish actress, Mme. Modjeska, who really convinced him. Perhaps she told him that it was his duty as a Pole to make the most of his talents for the glory of their country and so appealed to that passionate patriotism for which he was to become so well known.

Leschetizky, who was also a Pole, was never so famous as a performer as he was a teacher, though he played in public often and was known as a superlative technician. He was one of Anton Rubinstein's original associates at the Petersburg Conservatory, where he taught from 1852 to 1878. His long career continued in Vienna, where he established his school and taught until his death in 1915. He trained pianists of two generations, and some of the most dazzling performers of the time were proud to call themselves his students. These included Vassily Safanoff, who became a great teacher in Russia, Ossip Gabrilówitsch, Elly Ney, Annette Essipoff, Fanny Bloomfield, Ethel Leginska, Ignaz Friedman, Mark Hambourg, Artur Schnabel, Alexander Brailowsky, and Benno Moisewitsch. It was estimated that altogether Leschetizky taught eighteen hundred pupils, the great majority of whom became professionals of one kind or another. His methods were those of his teacher, Karl Czerny, though he had to develop additional techniques to accord with the advancements in piano building that had come about since Czerny's time. The pupils of Leschetizky's pupils must have amounted to many thousands. In his day and for years afterwards, there was no surer way to success as a piano teacher than to be able to advertise oneself as a pupil of Leschetizky.

Paderewski's real debut did not take place until he was twenty-seven. This was at Vienna in a concert given with the soprano Pauline Lucca, who was the operatic idol of the Viennese in those days. His impact was felt immediately, for he presented himself to the public as a fully mature artist. After debuts in Paris in 1888 and in London in 1890, he found himself established as a great concert star. Though he played in a wide repertory, his specialities were always Beethoven, Schumann, and, particularly, Chopin. His way with Chopin was different from that of the other famous virtuosos of the period.

At that time Rubinstein and von Bülow had reached the end of their careers, and those of subsequent masters such as Busoni and Rachmaninoff were just beginning. One of the most distinctive artists then and the one who most nearly rivaled Paderewski as a Chopin player was Vladimir de Pachmann. Trained at the Vienna Conservatory by Joseph Dachs,

who was a pupil of Karl Czerny, he was essentially a minia-
turist, a pianist of very different character from his contemporaries, the majority of whom were pupils or followers of
Liszt. We know from his recordings, made when he was an
old man of failing powers, that de Pachmann was able to create moments of exquisite poetry. His proudest boast was that
he more than any other pianist played like Chopin himself, a
claim impossible either to prove or disprove. He was greatly
popular in Europe and America for many years and attracted the public not only for his often beautiful playing but
for his eccentric behavior, which in his last years became
almost demented. He liked to talk to his audiences and often
stopped in the middle of a passage to comment upon it, or, if
it had pleased him particularly, play it again. Stories about
him are legion. A prominent conductor told about a concert
at which de Pachmann was to play a concerto. He insisted
that he could not do so without the music. So, at the performance, he appeared on the platform with a liveried servant who busily turned pages for him during the concert; but
the conductor noticed that the score de Pachmann appeared
to be following was upside down on the music rack.

Paderewski made his American debut at Carnegie Hall in
New York on November 17, 1891. Almost at once, he became in the minds of Americans the supreme pianist. He
gave 117 concerts on his first American tour. As a concert
attraction, he was of the same magnitude as Anton Rubinstein and Jenny Lind before him. In his own time, the only
other concert star who achieved such complete identity with
his instrument in the mind of the American public was the
violinist Fritz Kreisler. Paderewski was in the concert world
what Caruso was in the world of opera.

Like so many great pianists of history, Paderewski was an
ambitious composer and developed into a highly skilled one,
yet most of his music has faded from the repertory. Through
pianists undoubtedly will perform some of his brilliant piano
works occasionally, the rest of his compositions probably
will not be heard again. His most famous work, the Minuet

in G, enjoyed the kind of popularity that comes to certain salon pieces such as Rubinstein's Melody in F and Rachmaninoff's Prelude in C sharp minor. Nowadays, with radio, television, and recordings to provide home entertainment, the kind of performances at which such pieces were played so frequently hardly exist. Contemporary piano students have sterner tastes than their predecessors, and so the "light" repertory, which contains so many delightful things, is falling into neglect. Paderewski composed several brilliant large piano works that will always be of interest to virtuosos, though few of them have been given public performances in recent years. The best of these are the Variations and Fugue in B flat minor, op. 23 and the *Polish Fantasia* for piano and orchestra.

During his best years as a pianist, Paderewski toured almost constantly in Europe and America and also in South Africa and Australia. He spent his summers first at Aix-les-Bains in France and then at Morges in Switzerland. In 1899, he married Helena Górska, Baroness De Rosen. His piano concerto and the famous Minuet were composed in the same year. He spent three years working on a opera, *Manru,* based on a story by the Polish author Kraszewski and set in the locale of the Tatra mountains. *Manru* had its première at Dresden on May 29, 1901, and was produced in New York at the Metropolitan Opera on February 14, 1902. Though received with great respect and given several further productions in Europe, *Manru* never really established itself in the operatic repertory.

One of Paderewski's most ambitious works, a Symphony in B Minor composed to commemorate the fortieth anniversary of the Polish Revolution of 1863-1864, was played by the Boston Symphony. Lasting an hour and twenty minutes, this work was a symphony of heroic proportions, comparable in scale to those of Gustav Mahler. But it was not destined to enjoy the kind of cumulative popularity that came to the Mahler symphonies.

Paderewski's unexpected career as a leader of his country

began in 1910 when he aroused intense patriotic fervor by giving a speech at Cracow, the university city of Poland. This was at the unveiling of a monument to commemorate the victory of the Polish King Jagiello over the Teuton knights in 1410. As a result, Paderewski became a rallying point for the Polish nationalists, and his house at Morges became a gathering place for political exiles and revolutionaries. When World War I broke out and the cause of Polish independence came into prominence, Paderewski, the most famous Pole of his time, automatically became the spiritual leader of his country. Returning to America in 1915, he made appeals from the concert platform for aid to Polish independence and gave some three hundred speeches at various official gatherings. He also organized an army of 22,000 Polish volunteers that was trained in Canada. It was said that during the war years he spent his entire fortune for the cause. Certainly, the attention he drew to the issue of Polish independence had much to do with its eventual realization. He was his country's representative at the Versailles Conference and is credited with having persuaded the great powers to make his country independent. He returned to Poland in December, 1918, and was greeted as the hero of his country. The following year he was elected Premier of Poland and Minister of Foreign Affairs. This was an extraordinary and probably unparalled achievement for a musician. Though he was, in the circumstances, the inevitable choice as leader of the new Polish Republic, he was not really fitted, by temperament or experience, for politics. So, a year after his election, he resigned. It was said at the time that he recognized that his role was mainly symbolic and so stepped aside, but there is evidence that he felt himself inadequate in his dealings with the Bolshevist Soviet Union and could not stomach the kind of maneuvering that he felt was required of him. Then, too, he may have been shaken by an assassination attempt that was made upon him by an unknown revolutionary. Still, his accomplishments extended beyond the symbolic. He obtained the coalition of various political elements within the country that made a stable government possible and secured its legality. He also was responsible for the formation of a national army.

Having put politics behind him, Paderewski settled in California and gave himself up to intense piano practice before reappearing as a concert artist in 1922. By this time, he was a living legend and, though his playing was never again what it once was, he was a greater concert star than ever.

By this time, many younger artists had established themselves, and in America there was a dazzling array of star pianists available to the public. But, despite the competition, Paderewski remained the king, at least so far as the public was concerned.

During this period, the man whom all pianists regarded as their master and inspiration was Leopold Godowsky, who was a kind of latter-day Karl Czerny. His effect on the public in America was not comparable to his effect on fellow pianists, for his playing was supposedly so subtle that it was lost in a large hall. Famous for his wit, which was often devastating, he was the friend and adviser of most of the great pianists of the day. He was also a celebrated teacher and, like Czerny, made many transcriptions and arrangements that still are considered to be the last word on piano technique. In them, he extended the possibilities of virtuosity and made demands upon the player that only a very few could meet. Pianists have always been fascinated by Godowsky's arrangements, though they are seldom performed in public. Many of the master pianists of the time used to gather in his living room in New York and listen openmouthed while he played his latest fiendish arrangement of a Chopin étude or his *Pasacaglia* on themes from Schubert's "Unfinished" Symphony. In his time, the man who specialized in Godowsky's works was his son-in-law, David Saperton. In recent years, some of the Godowsky transcriptions have been performed and recorded, with great effect, by the American virtuoso, Earl Wild.

Of the many anecdotes of Godowsky as a wit, the most

famous is the one about his sitting with the young violin virtuoso Mischa Elman in Carnegie Hall during the debut concert of Jascha Heifetz. After Heifetz had been playing for a
while, Elman whispered to Godowsky, "It's hot in here, isn't
it?" To which Godowsky replied, "Not for pianists." That his
wit could be cruel is evident in the story about one of his
pupils who had been to hear d'Albert and complained that
he played too many wrong notes. Godowsky said brightly,
"I'd rather hear him play wrong notes than hear you play the
right ones."

The grand piano as we know it today, which has been
finalized at seven and a third octaves, reached its present
stage of development in the eighteen nineties. In 1900, the
invention of the pianola, which was developed by the Aeolian Company, resulted in the craze for player pianos that
lasted until phonograph recordings proved to be better and
more effective. By 1914, there were forty-two companies
making player pianos in the United States. Many a music
lover acquired his knowledge of the piano repertory from the
rolls made by the great pianists of the time for player pianos.
However, the mechanical process was such that much subtlety was lost, and the rolls that we have made by famous
players are not really fair to them. Still, they are valuable in
the case of players who made rolls but no recordings. Fortunately, some of Paderewski's recordings, though made when
he was past his prime, are good enough to show us why he
was so idolized. They convey that subtle and elusive quality
of personality. What he does in Chopin or Liszt seems beautiful, though we know that his mannerisms would be con-
demned in any other player. The rolled chords and use of the
hands not together but one after the other certainly consti-
tute eccentricities, but one forgets them as one listens. No
doubt, these were mannerisms of his later years. It can not
be said whether they were deliberate or unintentional.

During his last years, when he continued to tour, in Europe and America, Paderewski raised much money for the
relief of war victims. He also established a fund to stimulate

and encourage American composers. In 1936, he acted in a motion picture called *Moonlight Sonata*, not a good story but a fascinating record of the man and his playing. He did not have many pupils, but two of them, Harold Bauer and Sigismond Stojowski became notable artists.

In 1939, Paderewski was asked to return to the service of his country by succeeding to the presidency. He refused. However, when World War II came, he accepted the presidency of the Polish parliament-in-exile. Just before the war, he had completed his edition of the complete works of Chopin for the Polish Institute. He returned to America in 1940 to work in the interest of the exiled Polish government. His death in New York the following year came during a dark time in the world's history. It may have seemed to him that much of what he had worked for was lost. Still, though he probably would not have liked his country as it is today, he would find that his effect upon its history and its culture was lasting and profound.

Ferruccio Busoni
1866-1924

BUSONI'S parents were both accomplished musicians. His father, Ferdinando Busoni, was a clarinet virtuoso of definite if limited fame whose specialty was the performance of opera fantasias in which his clarinet reproduced the *bel canto* effects of singers. His musical training was far from complete and his talent was so individual that he was good only as a soloist and was never successful as an orchestral player. On the other hand, Busoni's mother, Anna Weiss Busoni had been thoroughly trained and was a first class pianist. Before her marriage, she had performed only at charity affairs and society gatherings in her native city of Trieste. Afterwards, however, she lived the life of a wandering musician, performing in concerts with her husband. Except for a brief flutter of success in Paris, the Busonis' career was routine and confined to provincial tours in Northern Italy and Austria. Ferdinando Busoni came from an old family of Empoli, a town between Pisa and Florence, where Ferruccio Busoni was born on April 1, 1866. Though Italian critics in later years often accused him of being a completely Germanized musician, Busoni was in fact a proud Italian whose great dream was to produce a truly nationalistic Italian opera. His mother was half German but Italian by tradition and training. Though Busoni did finally settle in Berlin and became Germanized in many ways, he always felt the call of Italy and returned there almost every year, even though Italian audiences were slow to accept him as a major artist.

Busoni's father was a difficult man, temperamental and improvident. His mother was loyal but sensitive and became increasingly dependent on religion and the devotion of her son. She was Busoni's only real piano teacher. Others were tried and promptly dismissed by his father, either because he did not like them or could not pay them. Both parents knew that their son was prodigiously intelligent and gifted. He began to play at their concerts when he was seven and by the time he was twelve was the only dependable support of the family. At one point in Busoni's childhood, when he was about twelve, the family was stranded for three months in the Austrian city of Klagenfurt because they could not pay the hotel bill. At thirteen, Busoni conducted the première of his own *Stabat Mater* in the Austrian city of Graz, then a music center of some importance. By this time, he had played in more than fifty concerts and had composed some 150 pieces. A committee of interested persons in Graz contributed enough money to the Busoni family so that Ferruccio was able to spend a year and a half studying intensively with Wilhelm Mayer, who gave him a thorough training in counterpoint and composition.

In 1882, after playing in five concerts at Bologna, Busoni was honored with membership in the venerable and distinguished Accademia Filarmonica. The only other musician to be so honored at such a young age was Mozart. The following year, the first of his nationalistic Italian works, a cantata, *Il Sabato del villaggio,* was produced at Bologna. It was dedicated to and conducted by Luigi Mancinelli, one of the leading Italian musicians of the time. On November 30, 1883, Busoni made his formal debut in Vienna, which was then the city where a musician of his background inevitably went to seek a career in music. His program on this occasion was typical of what was to come, being of heroic proportions. It consisted of the Bach *Italian Concerto,* the Beethoven Sonata op. 111, the *Andante Spianato and Grande Polonaise* of Chopin, several Liszt transcriptions, and several works of Busoni's own composition, including two *études* for piano, *Variations and Scherzo* for piano, violin, and cello, and the *Serenade* for cello and piano.

Though Busoni spent two years in Vienna, he was not happy there and in later years always returned to that city with trepidation. The intrigues among musicians and the general frivolity of taste did not please him. He found patrons who together gave him a small allowance for several years to come; but the Viennese public failed to be impressed by his talents, and he was too young and too awkward to make much of an impression in society. He found more congenial surroundings in Leipzig, where he lived for three years and made his living composing opera fantasias to order and writing musical articles for a Trieste newspaper under the pen name of Bruno Fiorescucci. He was forced to support his parents and to appease the ego of his father, who was always in debt and involved in some grandiose scheme. However, he was on his own in Leipzig, for the first time in his life, and able to struggle with the growing pains that are inescapable in youth and doubly difficult for musicians who must make the transition from prodigy to mature performer.

When Busoni's Quartet was given its première at the Leipzig Gewandhaus in 1888, it was heard by an audience that included the composers Tchaikovsky, Grieg, and Frederick Delius. It was at this time that Busoni met Theodore Steinway, head of the piano company of Steinway & Sons, who predicted a great future for him, gave him a small endowment, and invited him to the Bayreuth Festival as his guest. Busoni must have enjoyed the experience, but nothing at Beyreuth persuaded him to moderate his dislike for the music of Wagner. Steinway was arranging for Busoni to make an American tour when his sudden death put an end to these plans and to the patronage that, if it had continued, would have made Busoni's life very much easier.

In 1888, Busoni went to Finland to teach piano at the Hel-

sinki Conservatory. Remaining for two seasons, he found the
musical standards so low that he was unable to continue. He
was never to be happy as a member of the faculty at a conservatory, though he loved to teach, provided he could do
it his way. One of his associates in Helsinki was to become a
lifelong friend. This was Adolf Brodsky, the violinist who
first performed the Tchaikovsky Concerto after Leopold
Auer, the Czar's official violinist, turned it down.

It was in Helsinki that Busoni had the good fortune to
meet Gerda Sjöstrand, the girl he was to marry. The daughter of a Swedish sculptor, she was beautiful and intelligent,
sensitive and gay. It is doubtful whether many famous musicians had so devoted and sympathetic a wife, and her marriage to Busoni must have been one of the happiest and most
successful in musical history. Busoni had some difficulty in
reconciling his parents to his marriage, and it did not take
place until September 27, 1890, in Moscow, where Busoni
had accepted an appointment at the conservatory.

The Moscow experience was no happier than the one in
Helsinki, though Busoni's reputation was advanced consid-
erably when he won the Rubinstein prize for composition in
1890 with his *Konzertstück* for piano and orchestra. It generally was admitted that he should have won the prize for
piano playing, too, but the judges decided that it would be
unwise to give both prizes to a non-Russian. Busoni had already attracted the notice of Anton Rubinstein when he was
performing as a prodigy, as he had that of Liszt and Brahms.
Rubinstein was one of the strongest influences on Busoni
as a pianist, though Busoni's style, as it later developed,
differed greatly from the Russian's. It was said that if Busoni
and d'Albert could have been combined into one pianist, the
result would be the greatest who ever lived. A greater ap-
proximation of Busoni's playing might be effected by saying
that he combined the virtues of Rubinstein and von Bülow,
Liszt's pupil. Certainly, Busoni's idol was Liszt, whom he
never heard play. Like Teresa Carreño and Rubinstein himself, Busoni never studied with any great master and was

It was never really popular in Busoni's day but has been revived with increasing frequency in recent years. Busoni's
first opera, *Die Brautwahl* had been produced at Hamburg
five years earlier. His development as a composer was slow,
and he considered that his first composition of any real
worth was the Violin Sonata composed in 1899.

Busoni began the monumental task of editing the complete piano works of Liszt in 1902, and at the same time began a series of orchestral concerts in Berlin at which he conducted works that were either unknown in Germany or un-
justly neglected. He gave twelve of these concerts in seven
years and introduced to Germany works by Elgar, Delius,
d'Indy, Saint-Saëns, Sinding, Debussy, Sibelius, Nielsen,
Ysaÿe, Fauré, and Bartók. He was always particularly bent
on promoting the works of Sinding, Saint-Saëns, and Pfitz-
ner, composers he considered were not getting their due.
Busoni's first important première as a composer was in Berlin on November 17, 1904, when he performed his own
Piano Concerto, a gigantic work that is of extreme difficulty
and calls for a chorus in the final movement. This work, too,
fell into neglect, but, like so many of Busoni's works, has
been revived of late with great success.

In addition to his prodigious musical gifts, Busoni was a
talented painter and was particularly good at architectural
drawing. He also wrote a good deal and was a voracious
reader. He entertained ideas about composing operas about
Leonardo da Vinci and Dante but put them aside when he
finally settled on the idea of an opera derived from but not
based on Goethe's *Faust*. This work concerned him for many
years and was left unfinished at his death. The final scene
was completed by one of his pupils and the opera was produced posthumously at Dresden on May 21, 1925. Busoni's
Doctor Faust has been much admired by musicians but not
by the public, though recent revivals in Europe indicate that
it may find a permanent place in the repertory.

Busoni's two sons (the second, Rafaello, was born in
1901) both became painters. The musician's parents, Ferdinando and Anna, both died in the same year, 1909. They

spent their last years in Trieste. Whenever Busoni came to visit them and played for their friends, Ferdinando interrupted by shouting, "I taught him, I taught him."

In 1913, Busoni became director of the Liceo Rossini in Bologna, but this, like his experiences in Helsinki, Moscow, and Boston, did not work out. He went off on an American tour after one year and never returned to the post. The war years he spent in Switzerland. His return to Berlin in 1920 was celebrated by a concert at which he performed the *Hammerklavier* Sonata of Beethoven, the twenty-four *Préludes* of Chopin, and the Paganini-Liszt *Études*. His last public appearance was with the Berlin Philharmonic in the Beethoven *Emperor* Concerto on May 29, 1922. He died in Berlin on July 27, 1924.

During his last years, Busoni was surrounded by the chaos of post-war Germany. Inflation made living difficult. He was ill for several years, but continued to work on his opera, to perform occasionally, and to give his attention to several composition pupils, one of whom was Kurt Weill, the unique composer of *The Three-Penny Opera* and *Mahagonny*.

Busoni once went on record as saying that the only pianists among his contemporaries whom he could admire unreservedly were Emil Sauer, d'Albert, and Alfred Reisenauer. All three were pupils of Liszt. His other famous contemporaries, such as Carreño, Paderewski, de Pachmann, Rachmaninoff, and Hofmann, were not of the Liszt school. It was in the playing of Chopin that famous pianists were most frequently compared during Busoni's era. Busoni's approach to Chopin was not delicate but heroic. He despised sentimentality and bombast and was justly called intellectual insofar as he considered the emotional force of the composer to be more important than the emotional comments of the player.

Busoni made piano rolls but, apparently, no recordings. His style of playing was best exemplified in the subsequent generation by that of Egon Petri, the son of Busoni's friend the violinist Henri Petri, who studied with him and with Carreño.

As a composer, Busoni was considered too intellectual

also. But he was working against the fashion of the time. Just as he would probably rank as one of the greatest pianists today, his compositions are being revived and re-examined and have been discovered to be of surprisingly modern quality. It was no accident that Busoni was one of the founders of the International Society for Contemporary Music in 1923, for he was delighted with younger composers like Igor Stravinsky, who, he considered, were freeing music from the yoke of Wagnerianism.

As a person, Busoni was generous, robust, and witty (often bitingly so). His life, though it contained its share of problems and disappointments, was basically a happy one. That he was aware of this and of why it was so is evident from the last words he ever spoke. Taking his wife's hand, he said: "Dear Gerda, I thank you for every day that we have been together."

~17~

Artur Schnabel

1882=1951

SCHNABEL was one of those rare artists who sets his own standards early in life and adheres to them faithfully no matter what happens. In his case, those standards, though not generally accepted at first, eventually prevailed. He was not a reformer so much as a crusader among pianists.

It was apparent from a very early age that Schnabel had the fortunate combination of qualities—talent, technique, character, and intellect—that were necessary for the work that he set out to do. Though neither of his parents was a musician, he inherited from his mother the gift of absolute pitch. This rare endowment seems symbolic when the entire scope of his career is considered, for there was something of the absolute in everything he did. Born in the Silesian town of Lipnik (in that part of Austria that later was given to Poland) on April 17, 1882, he was taken to Vienna at the age of four. At six, he was accepted as a private pupil by Hans Schmitt, a professor at the Vienna Conservatory. His progress as a pianist was so remarkable that a prodigy's career was clearly indicated. The temptation to exploit him was removed, however, when, at the age of nine, he made a private debut, playing the Mozart D Minor Concerto, in the Gutmann Music Room and, as a result, was given a subsidy for seven years by a group of wealthy patrons. He also was presented with a Bösendorfer grand, which was then the favorite piano of the Viennese. With his immediate future thus secured, he was able to develop normally at his own pace.

Theodor Leschetizky had moved his headquarters to Vienna after many years in Russia, and Schnabel became his pupil at the age of nine. At first the boy was trained by assistants with only occasional lessons from Leschetizky himself. The great teacher recognized Schnabel's ability at once and appears to have realized that he was to become no ordinary virtuoso but something quite different. He was quoted as saying to Schnabel, "You're not a pianist, you're a musician." Since Leschetizky's business was the training of virtuosos for the international market, these words might have seemed disparaging. In later years, Schnabel remembered that the master often was very hard on him and, as a result, tried never to be hard on his own pupils. Yet, it was evident that Leschetizky was harder on him because he expected more of him. He knew that Schnabel must become a complete musician and so arranged that he study theory and composition with Eusebius Mandyczewski, a first-rate teacher and editor of the complete works of Schubert, Haydn, and Brahms. Schnabel met Brahms just before Brahms' death, and through Mandyczewski acquired his knowledge of and love for Schubert, the composer he was to serve so faithfully and well throughout his life.

Schnabel made his public debut at a concert in the Austrian town of Bielitz when he was eleven. Leschetizky thoroughly disapproved and forbade any further appearances for the time being, thus thwarting the plans of Schnabel's ambitious mother. The Schnabel family had moved back to Bielitz when Artur was eleven and he was on his own in Vienna, boarding with friends of the family. He did not perform anywhere except at Leschetizky's pupil demonstrations until January, 1897, when he appeared as accompanist to a well-known soprano. In the audience at this concert was Mark Twain, the American writer, whose daughter, Clara Clemens, was a Leschetizky pupil. She later married another

Leschetizky pupil, Ossip Gabrilówitsch, one of the finest pianists of his time.

The first full recital that Schnabel gave was at Bösendorfer Hall in Vienna on February 12, 1897. He was not yet fifteen. The program was a conventional one, of a kind expected of Leschetizky's pupils. It included works by Bach, Beethoven, Schumann, Tchaikovsky, Chopin, Rubinstein, Moskowski, Leschetizky, and Schütt. The public was properly impressed but not overwhelmed. Schnabel was at an awkward age and lacked the personal magnetism and flare that the traditionally frivolous Viennese expected from virtuosos. Leschetizky appeared to be satisfied; and it was evident that the time had come for the young artist to make his own way. That same year, Leschetizky offered prizes for piano compositions from his pupils. Schnabel submitted three anonymously and won all three prizes. However, he insisted on accepting only one prize and giving the others to his nearest competitors.

In 1898, Schnabel decided to go to Berlin, the city that then was the musical capital of the continent. His subsidy had run out and, at the age of sixteen, he was faced with the necessity of earning his living. He had a difficult time at first, though he captured the interest of Hermann Wolff, the impresario who managed a good many of the leading artists of the time. The official Schnabel debut in Berlin was at the Bechsteinsaal on October 10, 1898. After playing in Munich and Leipzig, he went on a provincial tour with a popular violinist. His second Berlin recital in 1899 was devoted to music of Schumann and Brahms. It attracted more than ordinary attention and marked Schnabel's break with tradition. From then on, he concentrated on programs devoted to extended works by a few chosen masters. However, he did not completely abandon a more extensive repertory for some years. Though his eventual fame came as an interpreter of Beethoeven, Schubert, Mozart, and to a lesser degree, Schumann and Brahms, he occasionally performed other works, particularly the Twenty-Four *Préludes* of Chopin, which were in his repertory almost to the end of his life.

Schnabel's first great love was for the music of Schubert. This was enlarged and encouraged by his association with the mezzo-soprano Therese Behr, an established *lieder* singer of great accomplishments. He was assigned to tour with her in 1899. She had been appearing in recitals with Alfred Reisenauer, a pianist far better known then than Schnabel, but soon arranged to appear exclusively with the younger artist, with whom she had an affinity both personal and professional that was to result in many memorable *lieder* concerts and, eventually, marriage. Therese Behr was five years older and eight inches taller than Schnabel and was a leading artist while he was still virtually unknown. She was the first to sing many of the songs of Richard Strauss, the most famous of German composers after Brahms.

The first of the many joint recitals by Therese Behr and Artur Schnabel, given at Königsberg on March 26, 1901, featured a Bach Fugue and a Schubert Sonata played by Schnabel and the *Six Sacred Songs* of Beethoven and the Schumann *Dichterliebe* sung by Behr with Schnabel at the piano. The two artists made their Berlin debut as a team the same year and quickly became established in the public esteem. The same year, Schnabel played his own Piano Concerto (a work in the style of Brahms) before an invited audience in Berlin. Wealthy friends had arranged the concert and hired the orchestra. The death of Hermann Wolff the following year created uncertainties for Schnabel's career. However, it received new impetus when he formed a trio with the violinist Alfred Wittenberg and the cellist Anton Hokking. They began a series of concerts at popular prices, given in a hall where beer was served between the musical numbers. However, these concerts became so successful that the tables were removed to make way for more chairs and no beer was needed to lure the public. Thus began Schnabel's long career as a chamber music player, during the course of which he performed with many of the great artists of the time.

Wealthy friends sponsored another private Schnabel concert in Berlin in 1903 at which he played the Brahms Second Concerto and a concerto by Paderewski. Therese Behr sang the première of his *Die Aussöhnung,* a work for mezzo-soprano and orchestra.

The following year Schnabel really arrived as a major artist in Berlin. He gave three solo recitals, four joint recitals with Therese Behr, appeared with the Bohemian Quartet, one of the outstanding chamber groups of the day, and gave a tour during which he performed the Liszt E flat Concerto, a very uncharacteristic work for him. In addition, he was engaged by the great conductor of the Berlin Philharmonic, Arthur Nikisch, to perform the Brahms First Concerto in Berlin and the Second Concerto in Leipzig. These great successes were strengthened during the same year when Schnabel performed the Beethoven *Emperor* Concerto with the Berlin Philharmonic under Richard Strauss.

Now that he was fully established, Schnabel was able to gain the consent of Therese Behr's father to their marriage, which took place in June, 1905. Thus began the happy relationship that was to last for forty-six years. The couple moved into a large Berlin apartment that was to be their home for twenty-eight years. Both the Schnabels began to acquire pupils and together they studied the *lieder* repertory. It was said that together they performed, either in private or in concert, all of the six hundred songs of Schubert.

Schnabel's English debut had taken place during his first great year, 1904, when he played the Brahms Second Concerto with the Hallé Orchestra at Queen's Hall, London, in the presence of Queen Victoria. Despite this auspicious beginning, he was not to become the revered artist that he did become in London for many years. After his marriage, he began the profound study of the piano works of the great romantic masters and abandoned composing completely for the next eight years. Though he had composed quite a few works, including many songs for Therese, he was not satisfied with them, and it was not until he had undergone a complete change of attitude toward composition that he took up that work again.

The Schnabels' first son, Karl Ulrich was born in 1909 and their second, Stefan, in 1912. Schnabel began his distinguished association with the violinist Karl Flesch in 1909. They gave many sonata recitals and trio concerts with the cellist Jean Gerardy and later with the cellist Hugo Becker. In 1911, Schnabel made his first Russian tour and in Hamburg gave his first recital devoted to sonatas of Beethoven. In 1912, he came under the influence of Arnold Schönberg, the revolutionary composer who had just moved to Berlin. As a result, Schnabel began composing again, this time in the so-called atonal style. His first work of this kind was a *Notturno* for voice and piano. Though he continued to compose in this vein, off and on, for the rest of his life, his works seldom had more than a single hearing and some of them were never performed at all during his lifetime. Strangely, Schnabel divided himself musically, composing in the most advanced style while he performed only the works of the great classical and romantic masters. Even his own piano compositions were eschewed by him and performed by others. This apparent dichotomy worked, however. It is entirely possible that Schnabel as a composer will enjoy a posthumous success when and if the general public acquires a taste for atonal music and creates a real demand for it, for his compositions are admired and respected by those musicians who know them and have the knowledge and experience to appreciate them.

Schnabel was unique among pianist-composers in that he never played his own works and performed his two roles entirely separately. The late nineteenth and early twentieth century was a period notable for the number of composer-pianists who, through their own works, had a profound influence on piano music and pianism in general. The list that begins with the extraordinary mystic, Alexander Scriabin, who invented the mystic chord built on fourths and composed sonatas that now are in fashion again, includes

Claude Debussy, Ferruccio Busoni, Maurice Ravel, Sergei Rachmaninoff, Nikolaus Medtner, Ernst von Dohnányi, Béla Bartók, Igor Stravinsky, and Sergei Prokofiev. Of these, only Rachmaninoff and Busoni were pianists in the complete sense. The others were noted as performers only in their own works. Rachmaninoff, of course, not only composed piano works that have become increasingly popular but was one of the foremost interpreters of the entire piano literature.

During the years of the first world war, Schnabel played wherever the German authorities demanded and often gave recitals of the Beethoven violin and piano sonatas with Flesch. Times were hard, and the only thing that saved the Schnabel family from actual privation were the tours he was able to give in Scandinavia, where he earned money in hard currency. He composed his first String Quartet in the year that the war ended.

It took a long time for Schnabel to become internationally famous. The public had to catch up with him, which it was willing to do at first only in Berlin and other German cities. His first American tour, which began in New York at Carnegie Hall on Christmas Day, 1921, was only mildly successful. His all-Beethoven recital at Town Hall three weeks later was praised but created no unusual excitement. He returned for another short tour the following year, but was discouraged and decided not to come back. He had an exclusive contract with the Knabe piano company and waited for its seven-year term to expire before changing his mind. Returning to Russia, now the Soviet Union, in 1924, he played Beethoven and Mozart to audiences that were eager but hardly receptive. During this tour he heard the nineteen-year-old sensation, Vladimir Horowitz, and advised him to leave the Soviet Union as soon as possible. Horowitz, took the advice quite promptly and soon was being hailed throughout Europe and America as the true inheritor of the Rubinstein tradition.

Schnabel's return to London a year later was inconspicuous. His first recital in Aeolian Hall was attended by only a hundred people. But the impression he made on those that heard him was profound and had important results later on. Schnabel by this time was completely dedicated to programs of long sonatas and other works by a few composers. He would play no encores, seek no publicity, and had no tricks with which to curry favor with his audiences. His manner was austere, almost severe, and he was very exacting about the kind of support he received from orchestras when he played concertos. Just the same, he was in great demand, at least in Germany and Austria, as a soloist with the major orchestras. All the great conductors of the day, such as Weingartner, Furtwängler, Walter, Klemperer, Szell, Busch, and Stiedry, acknowledged his eminence and wanted him for their concerts.

Schnabel was exacting about everything that had to do with music. He refused to return to America when the Steinway Company demanded that he play their instrument exclusively in Europe, too. Instead, when he did return to America, he imported two Bechsteins and a technician to service them. He also toured with his own piano stool, probably because he once had the experience of playing on one that slipped out from under him and caused him to miss the pedals. Finally the Steinway company gave in and agreed to his playing their piano only in America. Even so, Schnabel demanded and got many adjustments, for he found the Steinway "too loud" and "too fast" for his taste.

1927 was the centennial of Beethoven's death. To mark this occasion, many important musical events took place throughout the world. The most important, however, was undoubtedly Schnabel's performance of the complete cycle of thirty-two piano sonatas, given on seven consecutive Sundays in the hall of the Volksbühne in Berlin. This feat had never been accomplished before and has been but a few times since. Schnabel performed the entire cycle four times in all, twice in Berlin (again in 1933) and once each in London (1932) and New York (at Carnegie Hall in 1936). This was the fruition of many years' study, during which he prepared a new edition of the sonatas, published in Berlin during the centennial year and later in London and New York.

The inevitable conquest of London finally took place when Schnabel played the Brahms Second Concerto with the Royal Philharmonic in Queen's Hall on November 17, 1927. America capitulated in 1930 when he played (using his own Bechstein) at a Brahms festival given by the Boston Symphony under Serge Koussevitzky, appearing both in Boston and New York. He also performed the Beethoven Fourth Concerto at later concerts. Though Schnabel regularly performed all five of the Beethoven concertos, it was the fourth that seemed to be almost uniquely his.

Between his London and American triumphs, Schnabel participated in another unique musical event. During the Schubert centennial of 1928, he and Therese Schnabel gave a series of six concerts at which all the important piano works and song cycles were performed. This series still remains almost unequalled and was all the more important because the piano music of Schubert had remained almost unknown to the general public (and even to many famous pianists) for a hundred years. Though some of the shorter pieces, such as the *Impromptus* and *Moments Musicaux,* were familiar as salon music, Schnabel proved when he performed them that they were profound compositions, and he restored the great Schubert sonatas to their proper place in the repertory. From this time, Schnabel concentrated on Beethoven and Schubert and began his study of Mozart, who was probably his favorite composer and the one he believed was the most difficult to perform. Still he did occasionally perform works of Schumann, Brahms, Mendelssohn, Weber, and Dvořák, particularly in chamber music concerts. In 1934 in London, he gave another unique series, this time of music by Mozart, Schubert, and Schumann, playing most of their major works for piano solo in seven recitals.

After many years of resistance to mechanical reproductions of his playing, Schnabel finally agreed to record for His

Master's Voice in London. The series of recordings that he made, which included all of the Beethoven sonatas, began in 1933 and continued until the year of his death. He disliked the idea of recordings because he considered all of his performances to be different and none of them definitive. However, once he began he enjoyed the experience, as well as the added income, and was most exacting about the technical aspects, demanding from the technicians conditions that they thought impossible but which turned out not to be.

Paris was the one major city where Schnabel was unknown. He finally made his mark there in 1934. He also played again in the Soviet Union, in Palestine, Greece, and the Middle East. He played often in Italy and even tried to convince the Spanish that their diet of salon music was insufficient for musical nourishment. However unresponsive his audiences might be, Schnabel was always philosophic, witty, and determined. His American tours of 1933 and 1935 were successful enough to establish him as a major artist in a country that still thought of Paderewski as the ultimate pianist and of music as something to be taken in small and varied doses. Though many enterprising people had sponsored activities meant to improve musical taste, chamber music and solo recitals such as Schnabel gave were not generally popular in America until 1936, when the Sunday afternoon concerts of the New Friends of Music at Town Hall in New York helped build a public for music of that kind. Schnabel appeared at many of these concerts, both as soloist and chamber player.

The Schnabels were forced to give up their home in Berlin when Hitler came to power and began his anti-Semitic reign of terror. They moved first to their summer home at Tremezzo, Italy, on Lake Como. Then, after an Australian tour during which Schnabel gave sixteen recitals and appeared twelve times with orchestras, they settled in New York. Schnabel increased his composing activities and continued to teach, as did Mrs. Schnabel. He gave lectures at Chicago University and Harvard College. After becoming his own manager, he performed throughout America, sometimes in music for four hands with his son, Karl Ulrich. In 1944, he played five Mozart concertos with the Chicago Symphony. Two years later he returned to Europe, playing first in London at six concerts in the huge Albert Hall, the only concert hall left standing after the blitz.

The First Symphony of Schnabel was given its first performance by the Minneapolis Symphony under Dmitri Mitropoulos in 1946. It later was performed in London. His *Orchestral Rhapsody* was given its première by the Cleveland Orchestra under George Szell in 1948. The year before Schnabel had participated in the first Edinburgh Festival, playing the Beethoven Fourth Concerto and in chamber works of Mendelssohn, Schubert, and Brahms with the violist William Primrose, the violinist Josef Szigeti, and the cellist Pierre Fournier. He played at the Festival again the following year.

Beginning in 1948, Schnabel's eyesight began to fail and he was plagued with illnesses. It was thought that he might never play again, but he did, reappearing in Mozart concertos with the San Francisco Symphony under Pierre Monteux. Mozart had become his passion and Monteux his favorite conductor. After another illness, he performed the Beethoven Third Concerto with the Cleveland Orchestra and, in January, 1951, gave what was to be his last public concert at Hunter College in New York. In 1950, he made his recording of the Schubert *Impromptus*. This record, one of the most beautiful ever made, seems to contain all the beauty and joy that Schnabel had discovered in music during his lifetime. Though he was facing death when he made it, it is full of life.

It seems appropriate that Schnabel should die in Switzerland (on August 15, 1951) within sight of the great mountains that he loved so much. The standards of musicianship that he set have become those that now are required of every young musician. He, rather than the dashing warhorse pianists of the nineteenth century, has become the model. His pupils are teaching his doctrine in many parts of the world. Some of them have become performers of the highest quality, particularly Clifford Curzon, Lili Kraus, Rudolf Firkusny, Leonard Shure, and Beveridge Webster.

Though Schnabel was anything but a conventional virtuoso, he was a product of the Leschetizky school, which produced so many brilliant pianists. The Russian school, stemming from Anton Rubinstein, also produced many famous players, of which the greatest remaining is Vladimir Horowitz. It could be claimed that Van Cliburn, who won the Tchaikovsky prize in Moscow in 1958, also descends from this school through his teacher, Rosina Lhévinne, widow of Josef Lhévinne. Mme. Lhévinne has trained many of the best pianists of our time at the Juilliard School in New York.

Among contemporary pianists, Artur Rubinstein, the great concert artist who is still going strong at seventy-six, is probably the last of his breed. A pupil of Rudolf Breithaupt, he descends from the Liszt tradition, as does the veteran Wilhelm Backhaus, who was a pupil of d'Albert. Actually, the schools of Liszt and Leschetizky are closely related, as both originated in the school of Karl Czerny. So, it might be said of today's reigning virtuosos that Horowitz descends from the lion (Anton Rubinstein) and Artur Rubinstein from the eagle (Liszt).

So far as other schools of piano playing are concerned, it is beginning to appear more difficult to identify their adherents. The most important and probably the most distinctive is the French School as developed at the Paris Conservatoire. Pierre Joseph Zimmerman, Antoine François Marmontel, and Georges Matthias were the three leading piano professors there in the nineteenth century. Matthias was a pupil of Chopin. Camille Stamaty, though not a professor at the Conservatoire, was an influence on French piano style through his two most famous pupils, Gottschalk and Saint-Saëns. Another Conservatoire professor, Louis Diémer, taught many famous pianists, including the great Swiss virtuoso,

Alfred Cortot. The most celebrated teacher of the Paris Conservatoire in modern times was Isidor Philipp, a pupil of Matthias and Saint-Saëns. Philipp, who trained many noted pianists of our time, is credited with the ultimate development of the French school as we know it today through the playing of such remarkable artists as Guiomar Novaes, Robert Casadeseus, Jeanne-Marie Darré, and Philippe Entremont. Few indeed are the pianists who can triumph in the music of Debussy as well as in that of the classical and romantic composers. Artur Rubinstein has done so; and so did the extraordinary German pianist, Walter Gieseking. Neither was trained in the French school.

The Spanish school, somewhat influenced by the French, is founded on the highly individual piano music of four great composers, Isaac Albéniz, Enrique Granados, Manuel de Falla, and Joaquín Turina. In our time, a few outstanding Spanish artists like José Iturbi, Gonzalo Soriano, and Alicia De Larrocha have attained international fame as exponents of this unique repertory.

A great many of today's pianists have been trained by teachers of the school of Tobias Matthay, who was a product of the London Royal Academy of Music. He developed new techniques, many of them controversial and some of them contradictory to those of Leschetizky. His most famous pupil was Myra Hess, a great artist of Schnabel's caliber who shared his ideals. Though Schnabel and Hess were representatives of two schools that, for a time, were supposed to be in conflict, they were united on the highest plane of musical accomplishment.

At the present time, we tend to regard pianists as musicians first and virtuosos second, which is all to the good, though it makes a career as a pianist more difficult. The spectacular success of a Van Cliburn is rare today. The surest way to establish a career is to win one of the several major prizes for pianists. The annual Leventritt award, which entitles the winner to appearances with the New York Philharmonic and several other American orchestras, has brought attention to such distinguished young artists as Van Cliburn, Eugene Istomin, Gary Graffman, Sidney Foster, Leon Fleischer, and Malcolm Frager. The young Argentine pianist, Martha Argerich, has come into prominence by winning the Chopin, Busoni, and Geneva prizes. With so many prize winners and so many other young pianists of conspicuous ability, we have an abundance of talented artists of seemingly equal qualifications competing for the positions now occupied by the few remaining star pianists such as Rubinstein, Horowitz, Serkin, Arrau, Casadesus, Bachauer, Novaes, Michelangeli, Gilels, and Richter. Perhaps the day of the pianistic titans is over, simply because we now tend to take them for granted. Having such easy access to music through recordings, radio, and greatly increased concert activities, we can make comparisons that earlier generations could not. For a pianist to become a great star today is more difficult than ever before, for we expect everything of him. He must have personality, but he must be the servant of the music. He must be a virtuoso, but he must not display virtuosity at the expense of the music. And he must play nothing but the greatest music, which makes the greatest demands and allows for no easy expressions of personality. However, though the kind of adulation that was given to a Liszt, a Rubinstein, or a Paderewski is probably a thing of the past, there will always be a public for the really great pianists and even for those many who are merely very good.

As for the piano itself, it has come a long way and suffered many changes since Cristofori hit upon the idea of changing the quills and leather thongs that plucked the harpsichord strings, and the brass tangent that pressed those of the clavichord, for hammers that struck those of the pianoforte. Perfect as the modern concert grand now appears to be, further changes are possible. Several attempts have been made to develop quarter-tone pianos, and one that produces sixteenth tones has appeared. Early in this century, Paul von Janko created much excitement among pianists with his invention of a chromatic keyboard with six tiers of keys. They considered that it was the solution to many of their technical problems. Even so, the invention failed to make much headway. A few years later, Emmanuel Moor produced another novelty in his multiple-keyboard piano that was built for him by Bechstein. This too, though it attracted much interest, failed to catch on. Electronic pianos are in the making, and it may be that they will be important in the music of the future. We do know that music never ends, though it may at times appear to be doing so. And the piano, in some form or other, will survive, along with music, until the end of time.

Recommended Recordings

The Virtuoso Piano (Vanguard 1119) Pianist Earl Wild in performances of pieces by Henri Herz, Sigismond Thalberg, J. N. Hummel, Anton Rubinstein, Leopold Godowsky, and Ignace Jan Paderewski.

Keyboard Giants of the Past (Victor-LM 2824) Recorded performances by Ignace Jan Paderewski, Sergei Rachmaninoff, Olga Samaroff, Josef and Rosina Lhévinne, Alfred Cortot, Vladimir de Pachmann, and Ossip Gabrilówitsch.

Welte-Mignon Piano Rolls (Telefunken HT 32) Performances recorded from piano rolls by Eugen d'Albert, Teresa Carreño, Xavier Scharwenka, Emil Sauer, Frederic Lamond, Theodor Leschetizky, Alfred Grünfeld, and Ferruccio Busoni.

Domenico Scarlatti
Sonatas. Played on the harpsichord by Ralph Kirkpatrick. (Columbia SL-221)
Sonatas. Played on the piano by Vladimir Horowitz. (Columbia ML 6058)

Johann Christian Bach
Clavier Concertos. (Westminster 19096)

Muzio Clementi
Piano Sonatas. Played by Vladimir Horowitz. (Victor LM 1902)

Jan Lasilav Dussek
Piano Music. (Society for Forgotten Music SFM 1002)

Johann Baptist Cramer
    Études. Played by Miklos Schwalb. (Academy 303)
Johann Nepomuk Hummel
    Piano Concerto in B, op. 85. (Vox 12250)
Karl Czerny
    School of Velocity (excerpts). Played by Miklos Schwalb.
    (Academy 303)
Clara Schumann
    Piano Trio in G, op.17. (Decca 9555)
Louis Moreau Gottschalk
    Piano Music. Played by Eugene List. (Vanguard 485)
Ferruccio Busoni
    Indian Fantasy for piano and orchestra, op.44. (Decca
    10100)
    Fantasia Contrapuntistica. Played by Egon Petri. (West-
    minster 18844)
Artur Schnabel
    Piano Concerto. Played by Helen Schnabel. (SPA 55)

Performances by Artur Schnabel
    Beethoven. 32 Piano Sonatas. (13 records—Angel GRM
    4005)
    Schubert. Impromptus (complete). (HMV-1027)
    Mozart. Piano Concertos #21 and #27. (Angel—COLH
    67)

Index